Women, Law and Power:

Perspectives from Zimbabwe's Fast Track Land Reform Programme

Women, Law and Power:
Perspectives from Zimbabwe's Fast Track Land Reform Programme

Makanatsa Makonese

Published by
Weaver Press, Box A1922, Avondale, Harare, Zimbabwe, 2021
<www.weaverpresszimbabwe.com>
and
Southern & Eastern African Regional Centre for Women's Law
(SEARCWL)
Harare, Zimbabwe, 2021

© Makanatsa Makonese and SEARCWL, 2021

Publishing management: Weaver Press
Cover Design: Farai Wallace
Cover Photograph: by kind courtesy of Bio-Innovation Zimbabwe
Printed by: Directory Publishers, Bulawayo

The publishers would like to express their gratitude to SEARCWL for their support in the development of this text.

All rights reserved. No part of the publication may be reproduced, stored in a retrieval system or transmitted in any form by any means – electronic, mechanical, photocopying, recording, or otherwise – without the express written permission of the publisher.

ISBN: 978-1-77922-396-8 (p/b)
ISBN: 978-1-77922-397-5 (ePub)
ISBN: 978-1-77922-398-2 (PDF)

Contents

	Notes on the author	vii
	Acknowledgements	
	Preface	ix
1.	Introduction	1
2.	Zimbabwe's Land Policy, Law and Institutional Framework: From Colonialism to 2020	29
3.	Women's Land Rights as a Human Right	49
4.	Impact of Violence on Women's Rights to Access Land under the Fast Track Land Reform Programme	62
5.	Power and Law at Family, Local and National Levels	76
6.	Women, Power and Decision-Making for Access to and Control over Land	104
7.	Conclusion	138
8.	Bibliography	150

The Author

Makanatsa Makonese (née Nhengu) was born in Chivi District, Masvingo Province in 1974. She attended St Simon Zhara Primary School, Zimuto Secondary School and St David's Bonda Girls' High School for her primary and secondary education. She obtained a Bachelor of Laws Honours (LLBS) Degree from the University of Zimbabwe in 1997 and a Masters' Degree in Women's Law from the same university in 2008. Makanatsa holds a PhD in Law from the University of Zimbabwe's Southern and Eastern African Regional Centre for Women's Law, with a focus on women's law, land rights and international human rights law. Her research interests are in the areas of women's law, land law, environmental law, constitutional law and human rights law.

She has worked as the Executive Secretary/Chief Executive Officer of the Zimbabwe Human Rights Commission, Executive Secretary/Chief Executive Officer of the SADC Lawyers Association (Botswana and South Africa), a Senior Environmental Lawyer and Gender Programme Co-ordinator for the Zimbabwe Environmental Law Association, an Advocacy Officer for the Child Protection Society in Zimbabwe and as a Magistrate in Zimbabwe.

Makanatsa is currently the Deputy Chief of Party for the American Bar Association-Advancing Rights in Southern Africa Programme based in Johannesburg, South Africa. She has also worked with United Nations entities in Botswana, Zimbabwe and Uganda in developing national frameworks for the promotion and protection of women and girls' rights and the promotion of gender equality.

Makanatsa is married to Stanley and they have three children, Mufaro, Ruvarashe and Farirai.

North-South Legal Perspectives Series

Professor Julie Stewart, Professor Anne Hellum and Professor Patricia Kameri-Mbote (eds)

No. 1 *Pursuing grounded theory in law: South-North experiences in developing women's law* (1998). Agnete Weis Bentzon, Anne Hellum, Julie E. Stewart, Welshman Ncube and Torben Agersnap. Mond Books/TANAschehoug.

No. 2 *Women's human rights and legal pluralism in Africa: Mixed norms and identities in infertility management in Zimbabwe* (1999). Anne Hellum. Mond Books/TANO Aschehoug.

No. 3 *Taking law to the people: Gender, law reform and community legal education in Zimbabwe* (2003). Amy Shupikai Tsanga. Weaver Press.

No. 4 *Human rights, plural legalities and gendered realities: Paths are made by walking* (2007). Anne Hellum, Julie Stewart, Shaheen Sardar Ali and Amy Tsanga. Weaver Press.

No. 5 *Women & Law: Innovative approaches to teaching, research and analysis* (2011). Amy S. Tsanga and Julie E. Stewart (eds). Weaver Press.

No. 6 *Water is Life: Women's human rights in national and local water governance in Southern and Eastern Africa* (2015) Anne Hellum, Patricia Kameri-Mbote, Barbara van Koppen, et al. Published by Weaver Press in association with: Southern and Eastern African Regional Centre for Women's Law (SEARCWL) at the University of Zimbabwe and the Institute of Women's Law, Child Law and Discrimination Law, Department of Public and International Law at the University of Oslo.

No. 7 *Women, Law and Power: Perspectives from Zimbabwe's Fast Track Land Reform Programme* (2021). Makanatsa Makonese. Weaver Press in association with Southern and Eastern African Regional Centre for Women's Law (SEARCWL) at the University of Zimbabwe and the Department of Public and International Law at the University of Oslo

Herewith the presentation of the Series at UiO webpage.
https://www.jus.uio.no/ior/forskning/omrader/kvinnerett/publikasjoner/north-south-legal-perspectives-series/north-south-legal-perspectives-series.html

Acknowledgements

This book is the culmination of many years of my proud academic association with the Southern and Eastern African Regional Centre for Women's Law (SEARCWL) at the Faculty of Law, University of Zimbabwe. These years, and this book, would not have been possible without the guidance and support of Professors Julie Stewart, the Director of SEARCWL and Anne Hellum, Director of the Institute of Women's Law (University of Oslo). Thank you for holding my hand through my Masters' and PhD studies, for guiding the writing and publication of this book and for so generously reading the many drafts that I dropped before you on this journey. I would also like to thank Professor Patricia Kameri-Mbote, of the University of Nairobi, Faculty of Law for reading the final manuscript and for your constructive comments which encouraged me to think beyond the obvious.

I have lived a privileged life of being raised by two exceptional mothers; Betty Takaidza and Felistas Dzidzai Nhengu. Thank you for unreservedly believing in me and for telling everyone who cared to listen how proud you were of me. Your encouragement and love throughout my life gave me the drive to work hard and to push many boundaries.

My husband Stanley and my children Mufaro, Ruvarashe and Farirai, thank you for being my everyday cheerleading team, for the wonderful fun-filled days we have shared in our home and for holding me close when the going got tough. Thank you for giving me the space to read and write and for pulling me from my desk for a drive to the mall or a stroll on the streets of La Montagne to give me time to rest.

My late sister Rudo Belinda, I am certain that you are smiling from heaven, and pleased to see this book finally published. You were always such an inspiration, and you never hid the fact that you were proud of me as your big sister. The heavenly cheerleading team is getting bigger everyday with you, *amai*, *baba* and our brothers Munyenyiwa, Hokoyo and Thompson, applauding from beyond the clouds.

To my young sisters Sekai and Harugumi, my older sisters Ottilia and Bessie and my brothers Julius and Collins, thank you for being there for me and for reminding me every time that *"tiri vana vaTicha Nhengu"* (we are the children of Teacher Nhengu). Mai Tafadzwa and Mai Hesed, thank you for being part of this winning team.

My nieces and nephews, thank you for being my friends and for your interest in my work. This has kept me on my toes, knowing that there is such a huge squad expecting results from me.

To the Fabulous 40s, thank you for laughing with me, for crying with me and for keeping me sane as I juggled numerous assignments and the vagaries of life.

Last but not least, I am grateful to Irene Staunton and her team at Weaver Press, for painstakingly editing the manuscript and for the brilliant final product.

'Men should think twice before making widowhood women's
only path to power.'

Gloria Steinem

'To my two mothers: Betty Takaidza
and Felistas Dzidzai Nhengu.'

Preface

Growing up in my village, we had a very close relationship with the land and the natural resources found on it. I learnt to handle an ox-drawn plough before I was ten years old, to weed the fields and to harvest the crops, to guard the fields from the quelea birds and baboons and the occasional bush buck that would sneak in as soon as the round Bambara nut pods began to form. In good seasons, the time for *zhezha*[1] marked the peak of good nutrition in the village, with fresh food in abundance. After harvesting, we were assured of new clothes, school uniforms and shoes as proceeds from the sale of crops trickled into the household chest following delivery to the Grain Marketing Board (GMB).[2] Part of the money from the sale of crops was reserved for school fees and emergencies until the next harvest. In both the rainy and dry seasons, we picked seasonal wild fruits and gathered insects from the valleys and the mountains, which were a critical component of our daily nutritional allowance. We therefore always believed that as long as we had the land and the rivers, the grass and trees, the mountains and the anthills, we would always find something to eat.

By the time I was leaving the village for university in 1994, however, the land was showing signs of fatigue due to population increase, incessant drought and general environmental degradation. Instead of trees, there were bushes and shrubs, the rivers were silted and the wild animals that we once chased from the fields had become a rare sight. My male cousins and other young men in the village were getting married, and being allocated small pieces of land to build homes for their new families and to farm as per local custom. Girls would not be given land in the

---

1 This is the season when the crops are ripe in the fields and become an integral part of the daily diet.
2 The GMB is a state-owned entity responsible for buying and selling grain in the country and beyond. It was established by the Maize Control Act of 1931, recast under the Grain Marketing Act: Chapter 18: 14 in 1966 and given authority to deal in more agricultural products and their derivatives.

village unless they had children, or had been married and returned to the village after a divorce. Grazing land was being turned into fields and our playgrounds into homesteads. I worried about the consequences of these developments on my mother and step-mother (aunt),[3] who had raised us from subsistence farming following the death of our father when we were very young.

Many other women in the village had no other source of income and food, except from farming and the area's naturally occurring food resources. Therefore, when discussions about land reform in the country picked up momentum towards the end of the millennium, I was hopeful that the land challenges that people in my village were facing would finally be addressed, with more land being made available for resettlement. However, by the year 2000, the country's land reform programme was clearly taking a confused direction, and my hope for young people, women of my village and others around the country to access land were fast fading. It appeared increasingly likely that many who were supposed to benefit were not going to do so and that those who received land were unlikely to derive maximum benefit from it. When an opportunity for me to undertake research for my PhD thesis arose, I decided to research Zimbabwe's fast track land reform programme (FTLRP) and consider how it had impacted the women of the country, or more specifically, the women who had raised me in my village and the surrounding communities. I therefore went to Masvingo Province for my field research, hoping to better understand whether and how my community had benefitted from the FTLRP.

This book is based on both field work and a literature review, which was gathered as part of my research for my PhD studies at the University of Zimbabwe's Southern and East African Regional Centre for Women's Law, an Institute of the Faculty of Law. I undertook field work in the three Districts of Chivi, Masvingo and Mwenezi. I was born in the province's Chivi District and grew up in a village which I only intermittently left to visit my siblings in Masvingo, at Mashava Mine and in the capital Harare, or to go to boarding school for my O-levels at Zimuto Mission and for my A-level at St David's Bonda Girls High School. I subsequently left the village on a more permanent basis when I went to study Law at the University of Zimbabwe in 1994. So, more than twenty years later, I

---

3   My mother and step-mother were sisters.

treasured the opportunity to reconnect with my roots, as I undertook my field research in familiar valleys, farmlands, mountains, grasslands and escarpments.

1

Introduction

1.1 Introduction

As reflected in my own life, the land question has been an enduring issue in the history of Zimbabwe. From pre-colonial times to the modern-day post-colonial State of Zimbabwe, the land issue has dominated political, social and economic discourse. The implications regarding women's rights to access land generally, and agricultural land in particular have been immense. Given the long history of land and its political, economic and social impact on Zimbabweans, this book seeks to interrogate the land question in Zimbabwe with a focus on the Fast Track Land Reform Programme (FTLRP)[1] and how the policy and legal frameworks governing the programme as well as access, ownership and control patterns impacted the agricultural land rights of different categories of women.

The categorisation of women in this study is based on different characteristics such as marital and social status, political affiliation and age. It looks at the land rights of married, divorced, widowed and single women, farmworker women, young and older women, women as

---

[1] The term 'programme' is used throughout this book even though its use and meaning are often contested. I like many other researchers on the subject acknowledge that the initial phase of the process was chaotic, unplanned and violent. This would therefore not qualify as a 'programme' as it would imply that government planned the process from the beginning, which was not the case. The Supreme Court ruled in the case of *CFU vs. Minister of Agriculture Land and Resettlement* (SC132/2000) that the process was unconstitutional, in violation of human rights and could not be a land reform programme as contemplated in sec 16 A of the 1980 Constitution. It is, however, the term that has been generally accepted and used to describe the phase of the country's land reform and redistribution process that began with the widespread land invasions in 2000.

wives and daughters as well as women in different political formations. The underlying consideration is that when discussing women and access to agricultural land, women should not be lumped together as a homogenous group. My research focused on women as individuals but also as members of systems, societies, families and communities, and with the realisation that the discrimination that they face is not frozen in time, space or circumstances. At the same time, there is need to explore the collective discrimination faced by women because they are women and the differentiated discrimination or privileges that women experience because of their different social, economic, political and even marital positions. The comparison between women in different social and status groups is therefore useful in exploring the sameness[2] and difference[3] between women. This helps to explain how women from certain social and status categories may suffer from discrimination on the basis of their gender, their ethnic background and their socio-economic situation, leading to intersectional discrimination.[4] This will help in explaining why, when the FTLRP was implemented, many women were left out, and how and why the few women who benefitted manoeuvred a complex politically charged and male-dominated process.

1.2 Why the Fast Track Land Reform Programme

In this book, I interrogate the land question and women's access to land in Zimbabwe using the lens of the FTLRP.[5] This epoch in the history of Zimbabwe presented both continuities and discontinuities in the women's land rights conversation in the country. The former arose from the fact that gender-skewed land rights, wrought by the same century-old system, were not addressed by the FTLRP; the latter arose from the programme's stated objective to transform a century old, racially skewed land ownership pattern. As it dismantled the colonial hold on African land, the continuity of the colonial patriarchal systems that subordinated

---

2   The 'sameness' approach in relation to women posits that women are similar in all significant respects or characteristics to warrant them receiving similar treatment.
3   The 'difference' approach contends that women are not homogenous but have differences based on class, race, education, marital status, etc. It maintains that giving women similar treatment without taking their differences into account can create injustices and exacerbate inequality.
4   Article 14, CEDAW.
5   For the purposes of this research, a characterisation of what the FTLRP is will be provided in Chapter 2.

women and perpetuated their minority manifested through the postcolonial government's allocation of most of the land to the country's mostly black men to the exclusion of the majority women.[6] Laws to implement the FTLRP when they were enacted failed to specifically recognise gender-based discrimination in access to land as a historical disadvantage faced by women.

The book provides a multi-level and multi-layered analysis of the land question and its impact on women's rights to equality in accessing agricultural land. My particular focus begins in 2000, during which the FTLRP was initiated and ends in 2021 when this book was finalised. Throughout I consider the role of the law and the legal framework, in particular the received common law and how it defined land rights in relation to large-scale agricultural land to the eventual exclusion of the majority black population from access to prime agricultural land. The law also defined land value and gave titled ownership to the white colonial settlers, whilst confining the black people to the native areas/reserves (now called communal land), where the land belonged to the State and held no commercial value. In both instances, the subject of land and property was inescapably linked to the rights of men and their power and control over women. Women could only expect to benefit from land or property as appendages of their male relatives. As such, the cross-cutting themes in this book are law, power and the FTLRP and how these interacted to determine women's access to land relative to men.

For example, the challenges that women currently face in customary law in Zimbabwe and most of Africa regarding lack of recognition in land ownership and control, were similarly prevalent and widely recognised in European countries including Britain until the later decades of the nineteenth century. Research shows that in Britain:

> Married women were … legally considered subordinate to their husbands, and a woman's land automatically became the property of her husband on marriage. Married women were not legally entitled to own landed property until the passing of the Married Women's Property Act in 1870 and the Married Women's Property Rights Act

---

6   There was also no effort to identify and compensate individuals families and communities who directly lost their land and/or livestock and other property through the implementation of the Land Apportionment Act (1930) and the Land Husbandry Act (1969).

in 1882. However, single and widowed women were able to buy and sell land and participate in the 'outer' world of business, in contrast to the 'inner' world of the domestic household.[7]

Given that it was during this period that the colonisation of Africa was at its peak, it is not surprising that what was passed off as customary law in Zimbabwe and the rest of Africa and the relationship of women to land, was distorted to largely mirror the prevailing relationships in Europe at the time. In relation to the role of chiefs in land administration under colonialism, Cousins notes that 'In central and southern Africa, this 'feudal' model fitted well with British ways of thinking about states and societies. It also linked British land law and colonial contexts, and served the interests of regimes seeking to acquire land for settlers' (Cousins, 2008:8).

The interests between white and African males converged when it came to the need to suppress women and their rights, and the desire to maintain control over women and promote male hegemony in the social and political arena. As traditional leaders [and men in general] lost their land and power to the white colonial masters, one way of pacifying them was to give them control over women and children with the argument that this was in line with customary law and traditional practices. This led to the marginalisation of women in various aspects of their lives including in family relations and property rights such as land rights. Schmidt notes that:

> During the colonial era in Southern Rhodesia, African Chiefs, headmen, and other senior men, European capitalists and the colonial State collaborated in their efforts to control the behaviour of African women. Whilst African men sought to reassert their waning authority over women, their services and their offspring, European men had a different agenda. In the economic realm, they were concerned with obtaining cheap African male labour. If it took the regulation of female sexual practices to achieve this objective, the State was prepared to pass laws to that effect (Schmidt, 1992:121).

This viewpoint is shared by Chanock, who argues that:

---

7   University of Nottingham 'Manuscripts and Special Collections' available at: https://www.nottingham.ac.uk/manuscriptsandspecialcollections/learning/medievalwomen/theme3/propertyownership.aspx (last accessed 11 July 2020).

> But the African Law of modern Africa was born in and shaped by the colonial period. I think it can be shown that in the areas of criminal law and family law, African law represents the reaction of older men to a loss of control over wrongdoing generally and, as more acutely felt, to a loosening control over women (Chanock, 1978:80).

Effectively according to Chanock, the version of customary law that has been adopted in Zimbabwe and other African countries following colonialism was far removed from the customary law that was practiced in pre-colonial society. It was in fact an 'invented' version of customary law, which has been used to undermine the rights that women otherwise enjoyed in pre-colonial Zimbabwe and Africa. Building on this argument Banda notes that:

> African men, (in collusion with the white colonial governments) fearful of losing power and control over women restated a version of customary law rooted less in fluidity of daily practice but more in an assertion of a draconian version of custom that kept women in their places (Banda, 2005:18).

Other researchers on the development of African law such as Hellum's study of women's human rights and legal pluralism in Zimbabwe share the same view. Hellum, on the basis of court records from the Native Court of Appeal of Southern Rhodesia, observes (underlines) the independence that African women showed by running away from their male chaperons such as fathers, brothers and husbands to go to the mines, towns and mission stations as a threat to male patriarchal control. This led the African male elders and chiefs to collaborate with the colonial regime with the aim of regaining control over their wives and daughters with the help of the colonial State (Hellum, 1999:112). This control over women was not confined to their sexuality and reproductive capacity but touched on other aspects of their lives with the intention of making women entirely dependent on men.

The challenge in this collusion between the African men and European settlers was that, in colonies such as Southern Rhodesia, 'harmonising the African and European systems of social control became an exclusively European responsibility' (Mittlebeeler, 1976:10). This resulted in serious distortions of African custom and practices. The law-making process extended to women's productive labour on the land and reproductive labour in which they produced and raised labour for their husbands' families and for the colonial state. To achieve this, women had to be economically dependent on their husbands and the elders of the clan. One way of ensuring this was to deny them access to land in their own right whilst guaranteeing that they worked on their husbands' or clan land. Law-making on marriages was used to achieve these objectives. In the British Colony of Southern Rhodesia laws such as the Native Marriages Ordinance of 1901 and 1917 and the Native Adultery Punishment Ordinance of 1916 were used to control women's sexual and reproductive rights. Through the Native Marriage Ordinance, the marriage registration certificate was used as a pass document and women without the certificate could not be allowed on the mines, European farms or town areas. As a result, those without the certificate could easily be identified and sent back to their native areas (Schmidt, 1986:10). This meant that the movement of women was strictly limited and they could only move with the consent of their husbands, and in the case of unmarried women, their fathers or other male guardians.

The Native Adultery Punishment Ordinance provided that:

> Any native who commits adultery with a native married woman, or who induces a native married woman to leave her husband for the purpose of illicit sexual intercourse, or harbours her for the like purpose, against the will of her husband, shall be guilty of an offence, and upon conviction shall be liable to a fine not exceeding £100, or, in default of payment of any fine inflicted, to imprisonment with hard labour for a period not exceeding one year. Any native woman who is a consenting party to any of the above acts shall be liable to the like penalties.[8]

This law and its provisions were meant to give African men the satisfaction that if they left their wives in their native areas whilst they went in search of paid employment, their wives would be protected thus ensuring labour for the colonial state. The Attorney General of Southern Rhodesia, Mr Clarkson Henry Tredgold[9] in support of this law suggested that this was supported by the native males who felt that 'their whole family life is being disturbed and that they dare not leave their homes

---

8   Section 1.
9   Attorney General of Southern Rhodesia between 1903 and 1919 (Per J.P Van Niekerk, 2013).

in search of labour'.[10] The Native Registration Act of 1935 controlled women's movement, which could only be sanctioned with the consent of their husbands or some male authority, with the colonial government justifying this law on the basis of custom. This led to the confinement of women to the native reserves where they worked their husbands' and clan land and produced and raised the much-needed family and colonial labour. The colonial state also concentrated available 'native' land in the hands of the men through laws such as the Land Apportionment Act, 1930 and the Native Land Husbandry Act, 1951.

These controls over women brought together white males and black males, even though with completely different agendas (Schmidt, 1991:756). With economic interests at heart on the part of the white settlers and the need to regain control over 'their' women on the part of African men and traditional leaders, the law-making process was therefore effectively used in controlling women's productive and reproductive capabilities. The control over married women's sexuality and mobility became highly political. African men complained to the colonial authorities that their wives and girl children had become too independent and were running away with foreigners, mainly from the then Northern Rhodesia and Nyasaland who were settling in Southern Rhodesia in search of employment on the farms and in the mines, amongst other 'misdemeanours'.[11] Between 1903 and 1911 several Native Commissioners brought the dissatisfaction of the African men over their lack of control over their wives and girls to the attention of the national authorities in Southern Rhodesia stating in their reports the need for adultery to be criminalised. The Native Commissioners even postulated that adultery had economic consequences for the colony of Southern Rhodesia stating that 'the evil [of adultery] is becoming very wide-spread

---

10 See The Natives Adultery Punishment Ordinance (Zimbabwe) 1916. Criticisms by Native Commissioners, Matabeleland, on the Native Affairs Committee of Enquiry, 1910 no date, pres August 1911. A3/3.18.

11 Barnes, T.A. (1992:591) notes that 'By the beginning of the First World War, African male elders in rural areas were starting to voice their complaints about new, unruly female behaviour… In 1914 the chiefs and elders of the north-eastern towns of Rusape and Umtali were reported by the local government representative as saying, 'Our fathers have asked, we have asked, and you do not help us in the only thing that is vital to our tribe and our family.' They were pleading for restrictions on mobile women-girls who ran away from home to escape arranged marriages, and married women who… were defining new lives for themselves in the mines and towns of the colony.

and even influencing married men in regard to the question of seeking work away from their kraals' Mittlebeeler (1976:124).

By 1912 the government was considering legislation to criminalise adultery and by 1916 the Native Adultery Punishment Ordinance was passed. In seeking the passing of the legislation, the Attorney General of Southern Rhodesia once again appealed to the economic interests of the Europeans. He argued that the passing of the legislation would make the African man secure and encourage him to seek employment outside his kraal as he needed to be convinced that the government did not excuse the act of adultery (Mittlebeeler, 1976:125) and therefore that if he left his kraal, his wife would not commit adultery in his absence. In essence 'the pivotal point as it turned out, was the status of the woman, for the purpose of the Act was to control married women and not married men or single women' (Mittlebeeler, 1967:125).

The law was being used as a powerful tool of control, pitting African women against African men and African men against European men and the colonial government. To control women's sexuality, their productive and reproductive labour, they had to be starved of land, the main economic resource of the time. The concentration of land in the hands of male traditional leaders and male heads of households meant that women lacked economic independence. In the end successive legislative and policy positions during the colonial period made it difficult for women to own or control land leading to marginalisation of women in land related matters. Successive governments both before and after independence used traditional governance structures (Chingarande, 2009:6) dominated by male chiefs, headmen and village heads,[12] who protected male privilege in the name of tradition and custom. As such, a family-based land rights system, in which the male head of family became the owner of the land, was promoted by both the colonial and Zimbabwe's post-independence government. To this day, as Paradza notes, male dominance in communal areas (former Tribal Trust Lands – TTLs) is based mainly on the governance of agricultural resources (Paradza, 2010:24) and these include land, livestock, draught power and related resources.

---

12   Whilst addressing the 2012 Annual Chiefs' Conference in Bulawayo in March 2012, the President of the Council of Chiefs, Chief Fortune Charumbira, told the gathering that there were only six female chiefs in the country and that ten years previously, the country had no female chief.

Given this reality, I use the period between 2000 and 2021 to help understand the cumulative impact of women's unequal land rights and the political, economic and social issues that continue to disadvantage women. Given women's marginalisation in relation to land access, control and ownership, the question is: did this new fight for land in Zimbabwe through the FTLRP change the narrative for women and introduce the much-needed reforms? The FTLRP was touted as a programme to end historical injustices and address long-standing inequality and discrimination, including gender inequality and gender-based discrimination. But was the programme in any way primed to address such inequalities in reality?

A major intervening historical event during the twenty-year period covered by this book was the removal of Zimbabwe's president Robert Mugabe through a military coup.[13] Mugabe was the architect of the country's FTLRP, which enlisted support and condemnation in equal measure from both inside and outside the country. The general consensus, however, even amongst its critics was that the racially skewed land access and distribution patterns in the country were unsustainable. The point of divergence was often the manner in which the programme was implemented, in particular the violence and disregard for the law that accompanied the takeover of farms from the white minority farmers. The question of equity was however usually about racial equity, with little regard paid to other disadvantaging elements such as gender, political affiliation and socio-economic status. When the 'new'[14] political dispensation followed the departure of Mugabe in 2017, there was hope for more equitable outcomes to be realised. The white farmers who had lost their land hoped that the new government would either return their land or compensate them for their investments, whilst aspiring blacks, who had failed to access land during the early years the FTLRP, were hopeful that a revision of the programme would also help them access land. The 'new' dispensation began on a positive note, initially promising

---

13 Various terms have been used to describe this event in the history of Zimbabwe which happened in November 2017. Such terms include 'soft coup' and 'military assisted transition' whilst other people insist that this was an outright coup.

14 There have been many debates about whether the installation of a new president in November 2017 following the coup can be described as a new dispensation given that it was the same ruling party that continued in power and that almost all the ministers from Mugabe's government were retained in the new President's Cabinet.

to disentangle itself from some of the policies of the 'previous' Mugabe regime, including policies on agricultural land and land reform.[15]

Indeed, policy pronouncement and some level of implementation have been seen in this regard. government has reiterated its desire to compensate the former white commercial farmers for improvements on their previous farms (Matiashe, 2019).[16] In 2020, it signed what it termed a Global Compensation Deed with the former white commercial farmers, agreeing to pay $3.5 billion (United States Dollars) for farm improvements[17] on the acquired farms. Government also passed a law, to compensate former black farm owners and white land owners whose land was protected through government to government Bilateral Protection Agreements (BIPPAs) or Bilateral Investment Treaties (BIT).[18] It also instituted a Commission of Inquiry into Sale of State Land in and Around Urban Areas[19] and a nationwide land audit by the Zimbabwe Land Commission.[20] In all these efforts, however, the gender question remained largely missing. Some movement with regards to gender in land access was seen in 2020, when with the help of the Food and Agricultural Organisation (FAO) of the United Nations, the government under the convenorship of Professor Mandivamba Rukuni embarked on a process of developing

---

15 There is debate over whether the current governing structure can be described as 'new', and the previous one as 'old' given that the main protagonists in both governments were/are essentially the same people.

16 Between 2019 and 2020, government made what it termed 'relief payments' of about USD10,000 per farm to mainly old and destitute former farmers (see https://www.dispatchlive.co.za/news/africa/2020-06-02-two-decades-on-zimbabwe-takes-stock-of-mugabe-land-reform-legacy/). By July 2020, there were indications that the government and the former white commercial farmers had reached a $3.5 billion agreement for compensation for improvements on the farms (see https://www.bloomberg.com/news/articles/2020-07-08/zimbabwe-s-evicted-white-farmers-get-3-5-billion-settlement-bid). The question was where the government would get the money from given the economic challenges in the country at that stage.

17 The agreement was signed on the 29 July 2020.

18 Government gazetted the Land Commission (Gazetted Land) (Disposal in Lieu of Compensation) Regulations, Statutory Instrument 62/2020 with an objective to 'provide for the disposal of land to persons… who are, in terms of section 295 of the constitution, entitled to compensation for acquisition of previously compulsorily acquired agricultural land' (Sec 3).

19 The Commission was appointed on 1 February 2018 and was chaired by High Court Judge Tendai Uchena

20 On 22 October 2018, the Zimbabwe Land Commission embarked on the national land audit (see https://www.herald.co.zw/land-audit-gets-underway/)

a gender sensitive national land policy.[21]

1.3 Land as a locus for political and social contestations

Whilst land may be local and concrete, the process of land reform often translates into a very legalistic affair, attracting profound international attention (Ikdahl, 2013:169). Questions are asked and rightly so, regarding the legal processes that are followed in land reform programmes worldwide, the fairness and levels of inclusivity of the processes and the attendant human rights and rule of law approaches that are employed. In addition to the legal issues 'land reform is [also] a political process, which is influenced by many stakeholders, both at the national and international level' (Chitsike, 2003).

I will consider the existence or otherwise of normative national and international policy as well as legal or human rights frameworks for the implementation of the FTLRP. This will help in tracing the link between the FTLRP laws and the history of land law and ownership in Zimbabwe. This approach is informed by the narrative given above, which illustrates that the current land discourse in the country has been influenced by over a century of land policy and law making which created access, control and ownership patterns that have a bearing on the extant state of affairs. I, therefore, will provide a chronological but analytical account of a still unfolding policy, legal and developmental process.

As the deposition of the Mugabe regime rightly showed, national laws and policies reflect the dominant power relations and decision-making processes in any national context. This was shown by the speed with which the 'new' government of Emmerson Mnangagwa[22] announced its inclusive approach in relation to access to agricultural land, stating categorically that white Zimbabweans were as entitled as black Zimbabweans to access agricultural land.[23] Mnangagwa was quoted as saying, 'I am saying we should cease to talk about who owns the farm in terms of colour. It is criminal talking about that. A farmer, black farmer,

---

21 The author was part of this process, which was still ongoing at the time of finalising the book.
22 Emmerson Mnangagwa was sworn in as the President of Zimbabwe on 24 November 2017 following the deposition of Robert Mugabe.
23 See https://www.aljazeera.com/news/2018/07/zimbabwe-elections-mnangagwa-courts-white-voters-vote-180721220731456.html

a white farmer is a Zimbabwean farmer."[24]

In line with this statement, laws such as the Indigenisation and Economic Empowerment Act [Chapter 14:33] have been amended to remove the requirement for 51% ownership of all companies in the country except in the diamond and platinum mining sectors.[25] This was a major shift in policy by government given that the indigenisation mantra was born out of the FTLRP and the government's push for black economic empowerment. Allowing the white community access to land was a clear departure from the position that was taken by the Mugabe leadership which clearly defined a Zimbabwean as black when dealing with rights and access to agricultural land.[26] The position taken by the Mnangagwa government was also in line with the provisions of the 2013 Constitution which states that:

> Every Zimbabwean citizen has a right to acquire, hold, occupy, use, transfer, hypothecate, lease or dispose of agricultural land regardless of his or her[27] race or colour;[28]

The efforts to compensate former white commercial farmers for improvements and the BIPPA and BIT land owners for both land and improvements is in line with the provisions of the 2013 Constitution.[29] But until this time, the government had not made any meaningful attempts to implement these constitutional provisions. Thus, when the new government made the initial announcements on compensation, many people dismissed it as a public relations stunt.[30]

From the early to mid-2000s, the Mugabe government regularly

---

24 Ibid.
25 These amendments were made through the Finance (Number 1) Act of 2018.
26 Sec 295 (1) of the Constitution differentiates between indigenous and non-indigenous Zimbabweans when it comes to the issue of compensation for land acquired under the FTLRP. In other words, it distinguishes between black and white Zimbabweans; between Zimbabweans whose heritage lies in the country, or those whose families might have migrated from Malawi, Zambia, Mozambique and South Africa.
27 The use of the words his or her implies that the Constitution acknowledges that both men and women are entitled to land on the basis of equality.
28 Constitution of Zimbabwe, Section 289 (b).
29 Sec 295 (3) of the Constitution provides that 'Any person, other than a person referred to in subsection (1) or (2), whose agricultural land was acquired by the State before the effective date is entitled to compensation from the State only for improvements that were on the land when it was acquired'.
30 It was believed that the government was doing this simply to court foreign direct investment.

announced that the land reform programme had been concluded.[31]

However, even now, subsequent political and economic developments reveal that the land issue is far from resolved but instead marred by contradictions and contestations.[32] For example, following the 31 July 2013 harmonised national elections, the new Minister of Lands and Rural Resettlement, Douglas Mombeshora, reinforced the view that the land reform and redistribution exercise was work in progress. He then embarked on a series of policy and legal changes, including the promulgation of a land occupation permit and regulatory framework,[33] issuing new permits[34] and hinting on the implementation of a land audit. The issuance of new permits followed the promulgation of Statutory Instrument 53/2014, Agricultural Land Settlement (Permit Terms and Conditions) Regulations, 2014. This 'work in progress' was reinforced years later after the appointment of a different Minister of Lands, Agriculture and Rural Resettlement, Perrance Shiri, on 30 November 2017 by President Mnangagwa. In January 2018, the Minister stopped the eviction of a white farmer, David Worwick, from his farm, Dovermvale Farm after its invasion by a former Cabinet minister and other people.[35]

In addition, the constant fights by various individuals over farms,[36]

---

31 For example, The Utete Land Reform Commission in its report, indicated that in a meeting with the then Vice President Joseph Msika in 2002, the Vice President had suggested that the land reform programme had been concluded satisfactorily.
32 On 8 February 2016, the Minister of Lands, Land Reform and Resettlement was quoted in the media as saying the land resettlement programme was 'almost' complete but went on to say that an envisaged land audit might unlock more land for resettlement.
33 Statutory Instrument 53/2014, Agricultural Land Settlement (Permit Terms and Conditions) Regulations, 2014.
34 'New Permits for A1 Farmers', *The Herald*, 23 May 2014.
35 See http://www.thezimbabwemail.com/farming-enviroment/shiri-saves-white-farmer-evicted-ex-minister-farmer-says-grateful/
36 For example, in an article titled 'Zim land issues still a legal minefield' *The Mail and Guardian* of 30 May 2014 chronicled a fight pitting ordinary land reform beneficiaries, against a senior army officer and the son of a deceased senior ZANU-PF official over lot 15 and 16 of Earling Farm in Mvurwi, Mashonaland Central Province, which had spilled into the courts. One of the most talked about cases was that of the Zimbabwean First Lady Grace Mugabe's eviction of families from the Manzou Farm in Mazoe District of Mashonaland Central Province in January 2015 to pave way for a wildlife sanctuary that she intended to establish on the farm. The families had resettled on the farm during the peak of the chaotic farm invasions in the year 2000, only for them to be evicted fifteen years later to pave way for a more powerful prospective land beneficiary. In 2020, Mnangagwa's government moved to repossess farmers allocated to former President Mugabe's key supporters including Jonathan Moyo, Patrick Zhuwao and Saviour Kasukuwere.

beneficiaries, a court decision that resulted in a former white commercial farmer taking back his land and the return of a white farmer to his farm to huge celebrations by his workers and the surrounding community after his earlier eviction[38] are all indications of a programme in a state of flux.[39] The 2020 government efforts and passing of laws on compensation reinforced this view.

As the contestations play out, however, it is essential to locate women in these developments. There is need to determine how women have fared in and benefited from the countless programmes as well as policy and legal reforms that government has implemented. This is important in light of the fact that Zimbabwe has ratified and adopted international women's human rights instruments[40] and is obliged to protect the rights of women to access land on the basis of equality with men. Zimbabwe has also affirmed the equal rights of women by promulgating laws[41] to protect the rights of women. More significantly the country has a Constitution[42]

---

land-reform programme. Some of the senior officials whose offer letters were withdrawn included former Masvingo governor, Titus Maluleke, ZANU-PF Central Committee member and former Deputy Minister Shuvai Mahofa (later Minister of State for Masvingo Province), ZANU-PF Politburo member Nelson Mawema, former Chiredzi South MP, Ailess Baloyi, former Chiredzi North MP, Ronald Ndaba, and Major-General Engelbert Rugeje. (See 'Bigwigs booted out of Save Conservancy' published in the *Herald* of 10 September 2014).

38 See http://www.thezimbabwenewslive.com/business-44667-white-farmer-robert-smart-returns-to-lesbury-farm-in-style-as-traditional-leaders-led-a-cleansing-ceremony.htm and http://www.dailymail.co.uk/news/article-5206491/A-heros-welcome-white-farmer-returns-farm.html

39 In a case pitting a former white commercial farmer, Heather Guild, against two new farmers that had been allocated her farm, Irene Zindi and Fungai Chaeruka, High Court Judge Nicholas Mathonsi on 26 February 2014 returned the farm to the former owner because the two new settlers were not utilising the land. In his judgment, the Judge said that those farmers who were not using land obtained under the FTLRP should have the farms withdrawn from them. It was the first court sanctioned return of a farm to a previous white owner and was therefore a significant ruling.

40 For example, the Convention on the Elimination of all Forms of Discrimination (CEDAW) 1979, and the SADC Protocol on Gender and Development, 2008.

41 For example, the Legal Age of Majority Act of 1982.

42 Constitution of Zimbabwe Amendment (Number 20) Act, 2013. This was a total amendment of the former (1980) Constitution which was repealed and substituted by the 2013 Constitution. Different provisions of the latter came into effect at different times. Some on 22 May 2013, the day that the Constitution was gazetted. Others on 22 August 2013, upon the assumption of office by the President following the first elections after the promulgation of the Constitution as provided for in Section 3 (2) of the Sixth Schedule of the 2013 Constitution. In addition, the Constitutional Court as provided for in Section 166 will only be effectively constituted seven years after the

that asserts not only the rights of women generally, but also specifically places an obligation on the state to ensure that women have equal access to resources including land.[43]

Sec 17 (1) (c) of the constitution deals with equal access to resources for women, including access to land. This provision is however under the section on National Objectives, which raises uncertainty about the justiciability of the provisions according to some scholars (Magaya, 2016). I would however counter argue that the Constitution does not state that the National Objectives are non-justiciable and therefore the state should be called to account for its failure to act as required, if it breaches any of the provisions under National Objectives. In fact, the National Objectives must 'be protected by interpreting the wide justiciable rights' (Kondo, 2017:175) in the Bill of Rights so as to promote wider enjoyment of human rights by citizens. However, even assuming that this particular provision is not justiciable, Section 289 (c) of the Constitution recognises gender balance as a guiding principle in the allocation of agricultural land. This provision is in Chapter 16 of the Constitution which is entrenched and requires a referendum for it to be amended. This signifies the importance of the provision and the need to use it to ensure that gender balance in land allocation in Zimbabwe reflects parity in numbers regarding access to the same type, sizes and quality of land amongst other considerations as well as joint access between spouses and protection of such access.

This of course is a recent development, and the legal framework on access to land did not always provide for equality between men and women. Precise attention to an inclusive and legislated approach to women's right to agricultural land only began in 2005 through Constitutional Amendment Number 17 of the Lancaster House (Independence/1980) Constitution[44] through the introduction of Section 23 (3a). This amendment was made following concerted demands by women and women's organisations for their rights to be recognised in

---

publication date (Section 18 (2) of the Sixth Schedule).
43 Section 17 (1) (c), Section 289 (c).
44 However, even with the new provision on the rights of women to access agricultural land on the basis of equality with men, the ongoing conflict between women's rights and customary law was evident. The 2013 Constitution still retained former provisions that allowed women to be discriminated against on the basis of customary and personal law in all other applicable aspects of their lives.

land redistribution in the country.⁴⁵ I refer here to an inclusive approach because, as I will show later, under pre-colonial and colonial customary law, single, widowed and divorced women under Shona customary law were often able to access land in their own right. Using this customary approach, the immediate post-independence land reform programme also considered access to land by single and widowed women under the Land Reform and Resettlement Programme Phase I. As an example, under this customary law approach, married daughters who divorced had the right of return (Stewart and Tsanga, 2007:412, Peters and Peters, 1998:187) to their natal homes, where they were often allocated land to farm, build homes and reside with their children, if they had any.

Widowed women on the other hand were allowed⁴⁶ to retain the agricultural land that they were using with their husbands during the husbands' lifetime without interference from family and community. As the late Chief Jonathan Mangwende⁴⁷ said, at customary law:

> There is no estate until the surviving spouse dies. In the case of a widow, she remains, or ought to remain on the land and farm as she had done or she and her co-wives had done previously (Stewart and Tsanga, 2007:413).

These measures provided protection to widowed, single and divorced women regarding access to land and other resources. Married women, however, suffered more serious prejudices that inhibited their access to land in their own right as they were expected to access land as appendages of their husbands. Arguably, married women more than single and widowed women had to mediate their access to land on the shadows and margins of the law because of their perceived dependency on their husbands.⁴⁸ Divorced women also faced challenges, especially with regards

---

45 Essoff, S. (2013) chronicles how the women's movement organised around the land question, forcing the government to make concessions with regards to women and access to land.

46 But this was and has not always been the case: sometimes women were evicted from the land by the marital family. There was, therefore, a gap between what ought to have happened and what did happen in reality.

47 Chief Mangwende was then the President of the Zimbabwe Council of Chiefs and he made these remarks during a meeting between members of the Ministry of Justice legal drafting team and women lawyers during negotiations on the reform of Zimbabwe's laws on inheritance. (He died on 17 December 2013.)

48 However, as I will explain later, pre-colonial customary law still had a level of respect for married women's land and property rights through the *tsevu* and *mavoko* and

to accessing communal land that belonged to their husbands' clans. They also faced challenges with regard to equitable sharing of property upon divorce leading to loss of valuable agricultural land on which they depended for their livelihoods. This was because it was socially difficult for them to stay at their husbands' clan land/rural home after divorce[49] surrounded by the husband's family and relatives who would often show hostility towards the woman. These contestations continued to manifest during the FTLRP, reinforced by a prohibitive legal framework which inhibited women's opportunities at the beginning of the programme.

1.4 Relevance and aim of the research

There is a significant body of research on the Zimbabwean FTLRP, part of which has managed to establish the level of access to agricultural land by women under the programme at both national level (Utete, 2003) and in geographically limited areas (Scoones, et al., 2010 and Matondi, 2013). There is convergence on the prognosis that women did not benefit from the programme on the same scale as men in terms of quantity, quality and value of agricultural land acquired. The findings from Scoones et al. (2010) in their research in Masvingo Province showed that 8% of A2[50] beneficiaries were women, 14% in A1[51] villagised schemes were women, 13% in A1 self-contained were women and 15% in the informal schemes were women. At a national level, only 18% and 12% of the beneficiaries of the programme in the A1 and A2 allocations respectively were women (Utete, 2003:25).[52] The access levels were therefore not only low when compared to men, but women were more concentrated in the lower

---

mombe yeumayi concepts.
49 See, for example, the case of *Khoza vs. Khoza,* HC-B-106.
50 The Zimbabwe Land Commission Act [Chapter 20:29] defines A2 land as 'a farm held under a ninety-nine year lease allocated under the Model A2 scheme (the Commercial Farm Settlement Scheme, not exceeding the maximum farm sizes prescribed under Statutory Instrument 419 of 1999 or any other law substituted for the same) described in the Land Reform and Resettlement Programme and Implementation Plan (Phase 2), published in April, 2001 (as re-issued and amended from time to time).
51 The Zimbabwe Land Commission Act [Chapter 20:29] defines A1 land as 'a farm held under a permit allocated under the Model A1 scheme (villagised, and three-tier land-use plans with minimum plots of three hectares) described in the Land Reform and Resettlement Programme and Implementation Plan (Phase 2), published in April, 2001 (as re-issued and amended from time to time).
52 By 2017, statistics were showing higher percentage allocations as shown in the National Gender Profile of Agriculture and Rural Livelihoods.

value allocations such as informal schemes as opposed to the prime A2 allocations. Matondi (2013) and Hanlon et al., (2012) also reached the conclusion that women had not benefitted from the FTLRP as much as men in Zimbabwe.

As there is already a body of knowledge on women and access to land, I focus on identifying, analysing and understanding the legal, political, economic and social factors that prevented women from equally participating in or benefitting from the FTLRP. In identifying and understanding these factors, efforts can be made to ensure that future land reform, redistribution and reorganisation processes address the rights of women to benefit equally in the allocation of agricultural land in the country. Whilst land size in a country remains static, the population continues to grow,[53] so there will always be a need by government to revisit the land question, including the currently unfinished FTLRP and its consequences. Gender considerations in law and policy formulation and implementation will always be a key facet of any land reform, redistribution and reallocation efforts.

To achieve this overall aim, I focus on the following objectives:

i. To analyse the role of formal/state law, customary law, cultural norms and practices and legal pluralism (that is the interplay between formal state law, customary law and social and cultural norms and practices) in determining access to agricultural land by different categories of women in Zimbabwe under the FTLRP;

ii. To understand the role of power relations and how they determined women's access to land under the FTLRP;

iii. To analyse the role of family relations and consequences of marriage, divorce and death in influencing access to resources and access to fast track land by women; and to

iv. Understand the relationship between law, land, power and gender in Zimbabwe where most women farm their husbands' or other male relatives' land with limited independent access of their own and no security of tenure to the land that they work.

---

53 The population of Zimbabwe was estimated at 2,746,852 in 1950, 3,776,681 in 1960, 7,408,624 in 1980, 11,881,477 in 2000 and 14,862,924 in 2020 (see https://www.macrotrends.net/countries/ZWE/zimbabwe/population)

It has been noted that:

> In Zimbabwe most women do farm their husband's land but they do not have any form of title (deed or a customarily acknowledged right) to that land (Mutopo, 2011:1026).

FAO has emphasised that lack of tenure security affects women's role as food producers and as a result:

> Gender differentiated rights to land have implications on rural food security and nutrition as well as on the wellbeing of rural families and individuals.[54]

This has been a challenge throughout Zimbabwe's history, particularly after the advent of colonialism, as women were often treated as minors who could not own property in their own right and lacked tenure security. The FTLRP was – at least at face value – supposed to address these challenges and promote access to land by women in light of its stated objective of addressing historical imbalances in access to and ownership of land. However, this was not achieved as shown by the statistics above. There were many contributors to this state of affairs. One of these was the flawed starting point at policy level, in that in a country in which women constitute 52% of the population, only 20% of the available land was set aside for women.[55] This was the same percentage of land that was set aside for war veterans who constituted less than 1% of the population at independence at approximately 65,000 (Sadomba, 2011:69). The number of war veterans had naturally reduced further due to death by the time of the implementation of the FTLRP with Raftopoulos and Savage (eds) (2004:64) putting the figure at around 50,000 in 2004. Yet the war veterans, at less than 1% of the national population, were targeted to receive the same amount of land as 52% of the population.

Whilst women participated in and played a significant role during the war of liberation and therefore formed part of the war veterans' population, their numbers were small compared to men. As such, the war veterans' beneficiary category as a point of entry for women was clearly a disadvantage. In addition, the gender roles that the majority of women

---

54 FAO Gender and land right data base. Available at: http://www.fao.org/sustainable-forest-management/toolbox/tools/tool-detail/en/c/236793/ (last accessed 8 December 2020).
55 Land Reform and Resettlement Programme Phase II.

played during the war, such as keeping the supply lines open for the male fighters, teaching in the refugee camps and nursing the sick and war injured made it difficult for women to be recognised as war combatants and war veterans when it came to access to land under the FTLRP. As Chogugudza notes:

> At the end of the war, these tasks were seen to have been merely women's patriotic duty and not in any way equal to actual engagement in the struggle, thus making it very difficult for women to receive compensation since only those who had fought in real combat were being recognised (Chogugudza, Undated: 44).

The specific quota allocation for war veterans under the FTLRP was meant to compensate them for their role in the armed struggle. Unfortunately, for women fighters, the image of the war veteran was a male who held a gun in his hands. Many women who deserved to benefit were left out due to this characterisation of the war veteran. The policy and conceptual framework for access levels for women under the land reform programme was therefore skewed from the onset.

In addressing the land needs of women, there is need to ensure that women are treated equally bearing in mind that women are not a homogenous group. In addition, without addressing the social, political and economic issues that have a bearing on women's land rights, policy and legislative changes per se will not effectively address the problem. Thus, there is a need for a holistic approach to addressing women's rights generally and women's rights to agricultural land specifically. A multifaceted assessment and understanding of the issues that prevented women from accessing land on the basis of equality with men under the FTLRP is an essential aspect of this equation. This includes the fact that many Zimbabwean women, like those in many African countries, depend on land as their main or only source of livelihood for themselves and their families (Mutopo, 2011, Action Aid, 2015).

Without land, women in general and rural women in particular are unable to enjoy their right to food or economic development. The FAO estimates that about 86% of women in Zimbabwe depend on land for their livelihoods and for food production (FAO, 2017:35). A programme of the nature and magnitude of the FTLRP should have and must continue to focus on availing land to women, which in turn will help in the economic and social development of both women and the country. There should be in place a fully implemented policy and legal framework to address this.

1.5 Conceptualising Power and the FTLRP

Power as a term is often used and applied in different social, political and economic contexts, relationships and engagements. Power can be defined as 'the capacity or ability to direct or influence the behaviour of others or the course of events'.[56] Power and the exercise thereof can be both negative and positive in application and outcome. Negative power is seen as coercive and constraining and is often exercised by those in positions of authority such as the state over other less powerful members of the community. Positive power, on the other hand emphasises the capacity and capabilities of different individuals and actors. Such capacity may be given to the less privileged, less influential and marginalised in society through processes of empowerment (Andreassen and Crawford, 2013: 5, 6). Negative power implies keeping those in subordinate positions in check by constantly reminding them who is in control. On the other hand, positive power may ensure that the marginalised and vulnerable are able to overcome their status to achieve more for themselves and their communities through processes of empowerment and capacity building.

Power also comes in different dimensions and typologies, the understanding of which is critical in comprehending the relationships that exist between and among different people or groups of people in society. Lukes (1974, 2005) has provided a classical analysis of the three dimensions of power by categorising these as visible, invisible and hidden. All three are regarded as negative in nature as they exist in an environment where people are subjected to domination and often acquiesce to that domination (Dowding, 2006:136) either willingly or because they have resigned themselves to the subordination to which they are exposed.

Visible power plays itself out in public bodies such as legislatures, local government bodies, local assemblies, or consultative forums.[57] These institutions are expected by law, constitutions (national and institution specific) and principles of good governance to be transparent, fair and inclusive in the manner by which they manage the affairs that affect their constituent members, followers, supporters and others subordinate to

---

56 Definition from http://www.oxforddictionaries.com/definition/english/power
57 www.powercube.net

them. They are viewed as existing for the public interest. Decisions and policies that are derived from these institutions are supposed to address and reflect the diversity of their constituents in order that their social, economic and even political challenges are addressed. However, even with fair laws, clear decision-making structures and institutions and guidelines on decision-making processes, there is seldom a level playing field. Consequently, strategies for social justice that target this high level of power have to focus on the who, how and what of decision-making processes so that they are more accountable to the poor, the vulnerable and the marginalised (VeneKlasen, 2006:39). Often decisions that are taken through the exercise of visible power are influenced by invisible and hidden power; thus, their public face is only a façade for the invisible power that exerts its influence behind the scenes.

Invisible power entails the circumstances in which a comparatively powerless group's rights and interests are concealed by the adoption of dominant ideologies, values and forms of behaviour by the groups themselves – i.e. the internalisation of powerlessness.[58] This results in resignation to the *status quo*; an acceptance by the oppressed that their oppression is irreversible and beyond their control.[59] VeneKlasen concluded in relation to the three dimensions of power that invisible power is the most treacherous and insidious because it forces people to think in a certain manner resulting in the dominant viewing themselves as superior and the oppressed as inferior. As a result, invisible power determines the 'psychological and ideological boundaries of participation' (VeneKlasen 2006:40) by placing the powerful and powerless in their respective 'positions'.

Hidden forms of power are exploited by vested interests to maintain their power and privilege by creating barriers to participation, excluding key issues from the public arena, or controlling politics 'backstage'.[60] This way the powerful, whether people or institutions, maintain their influence over who gets to the decision-making table and what is put on the agenda for discussion (VeneKlasen 2006:39).

In addition to Lukes' three-dimensional approach, power can also be understood in terms of its typologies namely 'power to', 'power over',

---

[58] www.powercube.net
[59] www.powercube.net
[60] www.powercube.net

'power with' and 'power within'. Gaventa, explains these concepts as follows:

> 'Power over' refers to the ability of the powerful to affect the actions and thoughts of the powerless. The 'power to' is important for the capacity to act; to exercise agency and to realise the potential of rights, citizenship or voice. 'Power within' often refers to gaining the sense of self-identity, confidence and awareness that is a precondition for action. 'Power with' refers to the synergy which can emerge through partnerships and collaboration with others, or through processes of collective action and alliance building (Gaventa, 2006:24).

By improving the vulnerable and marginalised people's capacity and agency, 'power to' is a positive type of power in that it ensures that the poor and the marginalised can act on issues to improve their situations. 'Power over', where the powerful forces are able to secure the compliance of the less powerful, is negative power as there is domination over the poor, the weak, the marginalised and the vulnerable by the powerful, the elites and those in control of a coercive state, economic and social machinery. 'Power with' and its collaborative, social mobilisation and alliance-building nature is positive and helps in ensuring that communities can come together to demand their rights including participation in decision-making, choosing their leaders and choosing the battles that they want to fight. It also helps communities and different social groups to identify their common challenges and impediments to enjoying their rights, and encourages them to approach such hurdles from a collective position. 'Power within' is equally positive in that it empowers individuals and provides them with the means and the confidence to determine their capacity and potential to act upon the world (Andreassen and Crawford, 2013: 7).

In relation to the FTLRP, there is need to understand how the various typologies and dimensions of power played out. Some women engaged with the power and worked around its influences, while some participated in decision-making at international, national, community and family level in furtherance of their right to land. It is also necessary to analyse the spaces of power available during the programme and ask whether women had the opportunity to interact with actors relevant to the FTLRP in those spaces. If the women sought such interactions, were they able to engage as decision-makers and leaders or did they do so from the sidelines as outsiders? How easy was it for women to engage with the different forms of power that existed during the programme?

Gaventa's power cube is a useful analytical tool that I will utilise in assessing the dimensions and typologies of power as well as the levels, the nature and forms of power relationships, spaces for engagement and the actors and structures that women had to engage with at the various stages of the FTLRP. However, for most women, particularly those on the farms and in rural areas, there was limited international and national level engagement; indeed, this appeared to be a relational platform for the elite in the form of formal women's rights groups and organisations. For the local level A1 or A2 farmer, her engagements and interactions lay at the provincial, district, local and family level with limited national level engagement and no international engagement at all.

In order to make the 'power cube' relevant to my study and to Zimbabwean women under the FTLRP, I added other levels of power, namely: provincial, district and family because they played a more noticeable role in facilitating or constraining women's access to land than the national and international levels emphasised in Gaventa's original power cube. I noted that the original cube was used to analyse power within groups and organisations, while I also sought to engage with the concept of power at an individual level. This, however, is not to minimise the effect of globalisation in blurring the link between the local and the international. Indeed, I am acutely aware of the possibility of downplaying the role of this level of engagement for Zimbabwean women in general, and the women in my study area in particular in their efforts to access land. The need to include the family as the lowest level of power is informed by the realisation that gender specific power relations and contestations play themselves out in more private or 'intimate' spaces, hence the need to start the power analysis at that level while public spaces of participation may focus on contestations between local, national and global arenas as locations of power (Gaventa, 2006:27).

Figure 1.1: The 'Power Cube': Levels, Spaces and Forms of Power for Women in Zimbabwe under the FTLRP

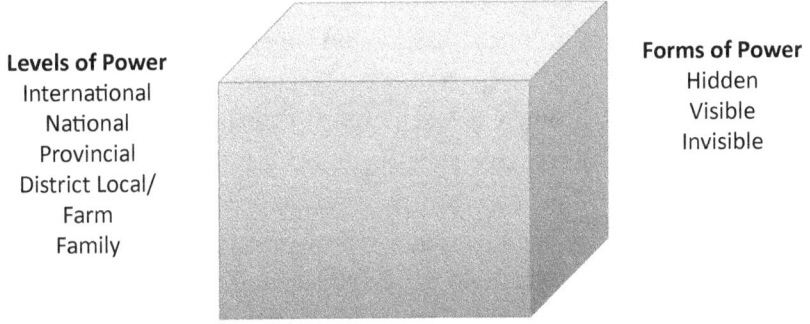

Levels of Power
International
National
Provincial
District Local/
Farm
Family

Forms of Power
Hidden
Visible
Invisible

Spaces of Power: Invited, Closed, Claimed/Created

Source: Adapted from Gaventa (2006:25).

The international level in the power cube has been retained in the analysis because power relationships at that level often had implications for women as they engaged with power and decision-making at the more localised level. Decisions that were made at international and national levels often called for implementation at the local level, so it was at these levels that women were affected by high level power and decision-making processes. Such decisions included policy decisions as made by the Executive and the passage of laws by Parliament to guide the land reform process.

For example, at the international level, the state reporting to the Committee on the Elimination of all forms of Discrimination Against Women (CEDAW Committee) has been an essential process with implications for women at the local level in Zimbabwe. This is because national women's rights organisations are involved in the state-reporting procedure. Furthermore, the CEDAW Committee often seeks to offer comments and observations that respond to women's rights claims in an effort to positively impact women at the local level and in relation to their lived realities. In its Concluding Observations to the combined 2nd, 3rd, 4th and 5th periodic reports by Zimbabwe to the CEDAW Committee in 2012, the Committee flagged the inequality and discrimination that women faced in access to land and other resources, including under the FTLRP. The Committee noted that despite the 20% quota reserved for women under the programme, statistics showed that only 10% of the land available was given to women.[61] The Committee called upon Zimbabwe as a CEDAW State Party to 'Eliminate all forms of discrimination with respect to ownership, co-sharing and inheritance of land' and to 'Monitor the implementation of the Land Reform Program to ensure that the quotas for women are achieved'.[62] Concluding Observations from the 6th CEDAW periodic report in 2020 identified the same issues, and recommended that government must 'expeditiously complete a comprehensive and independent land audit to ascertain land ownership patterns, expose inequalities in land redistribution and release land for redistribution to women'.[63] This showed that despite the CEDAW Committee recommendations in 2012, the issues of women and access to land under the FTLRP remained largely unaddressed in 2020 when Zimbabwe was up for review by the Committee. The CEDAW Committee picked the challenges and gave recommendations for redress, and government will be obliged to address the identified issues.

The implementation of these recommendation would provide a good example of international engagement with power resulting in local level implementation and advantages for women. The concluding observations were arrived at following engagement and representations to the CEDAW Committee by Zimbabwe as a State Party, and a shadow report by civil society organisations (CSOs).[64] The CSO shadow report is produced through a highly consultative process[65] and helps in informing the CEDAW Committee about the human rights reality of women in the country and therefore has a bearing on the ensuing concluding observations. It is clear that CEDAW reporting has the effect of pushing

---

61 Concluding observations of the Committee on the Elimination of Discrimination against Women, Zimbabwe, /C/ZWE/CO/2-5, Observation 35.
62 Concluding observations of the Committee on the Elimination of Discrimination against Women, Zimbabwe, /C/ZWE/CO/2-5, Observation 36 (a) and (b).
63 Concluding observations of the Committee on the Elimination of Discrimination against Women, Zimbabwe CEDAW/C/ZWE/CO/6, Observation 44 (a).
64 Organisations such as the Zimbabwe Women Lawyers' Association are often key in co-ordinating other CSOs in the development of the shadow report (see for example, GenderLinks' article on Zimbabwe's submission of its second, third, fourth and fifth periodic report in 2012 at https://genderlinks.org.za/barometer-newsletter/zimbabwe-submits-cedaw-report-2012-03-11/.
65 The report was produced by the Zimbabwe Women Lawyers' Association (ZWLA) and represented the views of ZWLA and 26 other national and grassroots organisations.

governments to action in order to comply with the women's rights dictates of the Convention as a way of pre-empting the reporting and the shadow reports by NGOs. State parties often seek to be seen as compliant both by the CEDAW Committee and the international community. Effectively this provides opportunities to raise women-specific issues and press for legal and constitutional reform (Stewart and Damiso, 2013:476) and illustrates the interface between international, national and local levels of power to bring about positive change for women. At the same time CSOs as a collective used their 'power with' to interact with visible power in order to achieve desired results for women.

1.6 Structure of the book

The books trails the role of law and power and how they impacted women's land rights under Zimbabwe's FTLRP. Chapter 1 is introductory. In this chapter, I share the objectives and relevance of my research in light of existing knowledge on the subject of women's law and land rights in Zimbabwe. I also provide a historical perspective of women's land rights from the pre-colonial, the colonial and post-colonial periods. I also discuss the concept of power, given its centrality in the book.

Chapter 2 offers a discussion of the country's land law and policies, their impact on women generally, and on women's land rights specifically. I look at the laws from a chronological historical perspective, starting from the country's colonial era and ending in the year 2021. Using this approach, I provide an analysis of the progress or otherwise of the country's law and policy-making trajectory in protecting women's land rights and their rights in other aspects of life as well. In Chapter 3 I look at the concept of women's land rights as a human rights issue, particularly from an international human rights perspective and how this framework can be used to protect women's land rights in the country.

In Chapter 4, I problematise violence as a means of power, and its persistence in Zimbabwe's social and political landscape from the time of the country's liberation struggle and throughout the country's post-independence political environment. I link the violence of the liberation struggle, the post-independence political violence and the violence that accompanied the FTLRP to women's failure to access land under the programme and conclude that the violence amounted to discrimination against women. Chapters 5 and 6 problematise law and power at various levels, including the family, the local, national and international levels and how power dynamics at these different levels impacted women's rights to land under the FTLRP. In Chapter 7, I provide concluding observations. The main observation is that the FTLRP has not addressed Zimbabwean women's land rights and needs. There is therefore need to rethink the current land reform and resettlement model and trajectory and use a human-rights based approach that is backed by the country's progressive constitutional principles to ensure gender equality and the protection of women's land rights.

2

Zimbabwe's Land Policy, Law and Institutional Framework: From Colonialism to 2020

2.1 Introduction

In Chapter 1, I drew attention to some of the family specific colonial laws, and their profound influence on various aspects of women's lives, including their family situations and access to land. The land specific laws had a similarly negative impact on women's rights to access, control and own land. However, the post-independence government also played a significantly negative role, especially in relation to its failure to undertake meaningful legal reforms to address gender inequality and gender-based discrimination as well as remove the repressive colonial legislation from the statute books immediately after independence in 1980.

The challenges faced by women in engaging with visible power during the law-making process in both the colonial and immediate post-independence period made it possible for the state to perpetuate the development and retention of gender insensitive laws. For example, it has been noted that 'The only interests taken into consideration in drafting the [Independence] Constitution were those of the participating males; the minority white settlers of the colonial government and the males representing the dominant parties involved in the conflict' (Ncube J., Undated: 3). The result was a Constitution that failed to provide the basic protections for women and girls in the country. The Independence Constitution did not even provide for the basic non-discrimination grounds to protect women and girls such as sex and gender, with non-discrimination on the basis of gender only being included in the Constitution through Amendment Number 14 of 1996 (Tsanga A.S, 2002: 221), sixteen years after independence.

The courts also played a negative role, especially in situations where they upheld discriminatory practices against women on the basis of customary law and other considerations. Court decisions such as *Magaya vs Magaya*[1] which upheld the customary law principle of male primogeniture[2] at a time when prior court decisions[3] and law reforms[4] had upheld the rights of women worked to delay the policy, legal and practice reforms in favour of equality and non-discrimination in the country. Earlier, in 1984, in the case of *Katekwe v Muchabaiwa 1984 (2) ZLR 112 (S)*, the Supreme Court in recognition of the progressive provisions of the Legal Age of Majority Act, declared that a woman over the age of eighteen years was fully emancipated and would therefore no longer require the assistance of a guardian in the conduct of her affairs. This helped in removing some of the discriminatory practices at customary law that prevented equal treatment of women. The decision in *Magaya v Magaya*[5] fifteen years later reversed the progress made in promoting gender equality and non-discrimination in the country. In passing judgment in the case Muchechetere J.A., concluded that:

> While women were given certain rights at common law under the Act [Legal Age of Majority Act] which they previously lacked, it was never in the contemplation of the legislature that the courts would interpret the Act so widely as to interfere with or distort customary law.

This interpretation was supported by the provisions of sec 23 (3) of the Independence Constitution, which at the time allowed for discrimination

---

1 SC 210/98
2 Dictates that the eldest male legitimate child of a deceased person is the one entitled to inherit.
3 *Katekwe v Muchabaiwa 1984 (2) ZLR 112 (S)*.
4 Such as the Legal Age of Majority Act, 1982.
5 Notably, the problematic elements of the decision regarding women's inheritance at customary law had already been addressed through the Administration of Estates Amendment Act, Number 6 of 1997 (sec 68) prior to the delivery of the judgement in *Magaya v Magaya*. However the facts in the Magaya case had arisen prior to the amendment of the law. Unfortunately, the Magaya decision distorted peoples' understanding of the actual legal position on intestate inheritance rights of women under customary law that should have prevailed in deceased estates under customary law as of 1 November 1997.

on the basis of customary law by stating that:

> Nothing contained in any law shall be held to be in contravention of subsection (1) (a) [the non-discrimination clause] to the extent that the law in question relates to any of the following matters – matters of personal law; [and]… the application of African customary law.

Effectively therefore, the law was giving with one hand, and taking back with another, in that whilst prohibiting discrimination, the above 'claw-back' clause provided for exceptions under which discrimination was allowed. The passing of progressive legislation without addressing the fundamental provisions on equality and non-discrimination in the Constitution effectively changed little for women in a country where customary laws and practices are held with approbation. To the credit of Zimbabweans, sec 23 (3) of the Independence Constitution was unequivocally repealed when the 2013 Constitution was promulgated with a provision that states that 'All laws, customs, traditions and cultural practices that infringe the rights of women conferred by this Constitution are void to the extent of the infringement'.[6]

In addition sec 56 (3) of the 2013 Constitution states that 'Every person has the right not to be treated in an unfairly discriminatory manner on such grounds as their… custom, culture, sex, gender…' In this regard, the country has come far in providing for the formal protection of women from inequality and discrimination, even though the substantive enjoyment of the protected rights remains largely a fantasy.

Before reaching this stage in the law-making process, there were various challenges that the women of the country had to contend with and in reality continue to grapple with. Damiso and Stewart, (2013:456) note that equality between men and women in Zimbabwe remains incomplete due to pervasive cultural relativism and the colonial history of the country. In particular the white colonialists did not give black women equal rights with black men due to a perceived cultural resistance from men. This was a political consideration as the colonialists feared that promotion of women's rights would lead to rebellion against the colonial government by the men (Damiso and Stewart, 2013: 456). The desire for political power by the colonial government and that for control over women by the African men led to a marriage of convenience between

---

6   Constitution of Zimbabwe, 2013, sec 80 (3).

African and European men leading to a wrong practice that viewed women as 'perpetual minors' being passed off as an African customary way of life (Jeater, 1993:85).

The colonially bestowed perpetual minority of women meant that they remained the responsibility of one or other male guardian, be it their father, husband, son or uncle and could not attain economic, social or personal independence. They therefore required the consent of their guardian to get married, whilst their economic assets effectively belonged to their guardian. This mutilated version of customary law, whether codified or uncodified is today more often than not the version that is used in dealing with the issue of women's rights to property at customary law as opposed to the progressive version, or the pragmatic approach taken in daily lives which often gives women power, authority and autonomy to own and control property including land. In her 1999 research, Hellum noted that in Africa the dual colonial legal system with its differentiated application for indigenous and European people in the area of personal law was gradually disappearing (Hellum, 1999:126), especially at a formal level through statutory and court interventions. In its Concluding Observations on the Sixth Periodic Report for Zimbabwe in 2020, the CEDAW Committee noted that despite the existence of a progressive constitution, customary laws and practices were still not in conformity with the Constitution and called on the government to address these anomalies (CEDAW Committee Report, 2020).

As such, at a practical and implementation level, the problem of discrimination against women remains. The result is that, even with the recent constitutional and statutory enactments seeking to subordinate customary law to human rights and the Constitution,[7] women still face considerable discrimination. This is based on erroneous interpretations of customary law and the invisible power that ensures that women embrace customary and cultural practices that oppress them. This invisible power also allows men to use the same practices to amplify their power and control over women despite the existence of laws that seek to support and protect women's rights.

---

7   Section 63 (b) of the 2013 Constitution whilst recognising everyone's right to participate in the cultural life of their choice emphasises that the enjoyment of such a right must not infringe the provisions of the Constitution.

2.2 Women and Ownership of Property at Customary Law

Contrary to general assumptions about women's lack of or limited rights in customary law, within traditional Shona customary law, a woman and not a man was allowed to individually own property and had sole control over such property throughout her lifetime (Gudhlanga and Makaudze, 2012:11). Although men owned and controlled considerable property, it was viewed as being owned or controlled on behalf of families, clans and communities.[8] On the other hand, women's property was owned by women in their individual capacity and in their own right. Such property was derived from or grown through *mombe yeumai*[9] and *mavoko*[10] property amongst others, both of which recognised the woman's efforts, often sole, in the acquisition of such property.

Early European hunters and adventurers recorded the active role that women played in the economic activities of pre-colonial Rhodesia. They were key players in the agricultural sector, in gold production and 'were also highly respected artisans and skilled workers, predominating in such trades as the moulding and burning of pots, beer brewing, midwifery, salt production, and herbalism' (Schmidt, 1988:56). The wealth from such activities was critical in further expanding family wealth and supporting the family's social standing. For example, it was used to pay bride wealth for their sons and brothers, and even to get more wives for their husbands. More wives and many children in turn meant more labour for the family, increased production and improved economic and social standing. As a result, women had considerable respect within their communities, and

---

8   This is why customary inheritance law dictated that a man inherited a deceased male relative's property not as his sole property but in trust for the dependents of the deceased.

9   Traditionally, this is a cow that is given to a woman by her son-in-law upon the marriage of her daughter. It is a token of appreciation by him to his mother-in-law for giving birth to and raising the daughter (his wife). The cow and its progeny are the woman's sole property over which she has total control. It is often believed that using *mombe yeumai* by the woman's husband's family or her children without her authority can lead to avenging spirits if she dies before it is replaced. Upon her death, in the absence of a will, the woman's natal family has absolute powers to determine how the cow, its progeny and related property will devolve.

10 *Mavoko* property is property derived through the woman's skills such as midwifery, pottery making, weaving and traditional healing. The property acquired in this way was traditionally treated the same way as *mombe yeumai* with the woman and her natal family in the event of her death having absolute authority and control over the property.

played an advisory and decision-making role in the family, including the families of their brothers. The respect given to the sister in relation to her brother's family exists even today in Shona culture because the sister is still expected to pay for her brother's *roora*.[11]

According to Mester, in Shona culture:

> Sisters are highly respected authorities in their brother's marriage, they are acting as advocates of their natal families vis-à-vis their brother's wives… The bargaining power of lineage sisters exists due to the paring of brother and sister in respect of bride price cattle. Because it is a sister, who brings the cattle for her brother's marriage into the family, she is in a position of authority in his family. For her brother's wife, she is *[v]amwene* (owner of the wife). His children call her *[v]atete*, a term expressing authority and a close emotional bond (Mester, 2008:1).

The respect that women commanded from their families and kith and kin was thus tied to the property that they owned or to which they contributed, whether through the work of their hands *(mavoko)* or property that came into the family through their own marriages *(roora)* or marriage of their daughters *(umai)*.

It was only with the advent of colonialism that all African women were regarded as perpetual minors and therefore incapable of owning property in their own right. As Beneria and Sen argue, European colonial rule, 'rather than being a 'liberalizing' factor for African women, contributed to their loss of status' (Beneria and Sen, 1981: 280-281). Consequently, the colonial system had little consideration for female agricultural systems resulting in the land reforms that were introduced by colonialism divesting women of their land rights as the settlers viewed land ownership and agriculture as a men's preserve (Beneria and Sen, 1981: 281).

Peters and Peters note that:

> The land and income rights Shona and Ndebele women enjoyed in pre-colonial communities, however, were threatened by foreign intervention into African societies. Settler colonialism in Southern Rhodesia (Zimbabwe) served to compromise the rights of women in Shona and Ndebele societies, as policies privileged male landholders

---

11   Bride price.

rather than Shona and Ndebele female farmers. (Peters and Peters, 1998:187-188).

In addition to land, any property that women acquired or contributed in acquiring was regarded as the husband's property resulting in their work, roles and efforts not being accorded individual recognition. This of course, as shown above, was far removed from customary law and the position of women with regards to ownership of property and access to land. With regards to land specifically, married women were always allocated pieces of land called *tsevu/tseu* in Shona and *isivande* in Ndebele within the bigger family landholding where they grew crops that they solely controlled. This was in recognition of the women's rights to agricultural land.[12] Essof notes that:

> Land rights in traditional communities were conferred upon marriage to a family unit and not to individuals, thus land was guaranteed to every adult individual sufficient for their needs. Women's rights to land were particularly protected through the *tsevu* or *isivande* concept (Essof, 2013).

These narratives show that Zimbabwean women's demands to be accorded rights to equality and non-discrimination generally and equal treatment in accessing land specifically is not an alien demand, but squarely lies within Zimbabwean customary law and culture. Unfortunately, as the following section will show, it was the distorted customary law as developed during the colonial period that was used by successive governments in making land laws and defining the position of women with regards to land, property and other life changing aspects including marriage.

2.3 The influence of colonial customary law on policy making and women's land rights

In Chapter 1, I outlined the colonial approach to customary law and how it was used to control women and girls' productive and reproductive lives, particularly within the family setting. This approach was subsequently embraced and used at policy and law-making levels by successive colonial and post-colonial governments. This influenced not only customary

---

12 It can, however, be argued that this concept was still not equitable in that married women were allocated a very small portion in the larger family landholding.

law but general law as well, given that even as the black Zimbabwean population embraced the colonial laws and way of life, they were not totally divorced from their customary ways of life, in particular those that entrenched patriarchy and subordinated women to the rule of fathers, husbands and other males. In essence, black Zimbabweans were operating and continue to operate under a conflated pluralist legal system.

The colonial and post-colonial legislation therefore pushed a view that customary law did not provide for women's rights to land, and in the general law realm in relation to the white population, there were limited attempts to accord women substantive equality and control of their lives, including opportunities to own and control property. For example, laws such as the Married Persons Property Act: Chapter 5:12 for a long time after colonisation of the then Southern Rhodesia provided for the doctrine of marital power in all marriages in community of property, including white marriages. The Act provided that the man in a marriage in community of property was in charge of the marital estate. The default in community of property marriage regime was only abolished in 1929, when civil marriages were legislated to be out of community of property unless the parties opted otherwise. However, for those that opted through an ante-nuptial contract to get married in community of property, the husband's authority over the marital estate remained. The desire to control women and their property rights was therefore not necessarily a customary law issue, but a patriarchal precept.

From a customary law perspective, the 1980 Constitution and its provisions allowing for discrimination on the basis of customary or personal law had a profound and negative effect on women's enjoyment of their property rights. The effects of such legal provisions were different for different categories of women. For example, married women in post-independence Zimbabwe were often required to live in the shadows of their husbands and to access resources such as land through their husbands as a result of such legal provisions.[13] There was a continuity of a system of law that infringed on women's rights through upholding discriminatory practices and justifying them on the basis of customary

---

13 For example, the immediate post-independence land reform programme focused on providing land to single (unmarried, widowed, divorced) women whilst married women were expected to access land through their husbands as the heads of households.

law. The continuation of the discriminatory practices took place despite a significant discontinuity occasioned by the transition of the country from colonialism to independence.

To date, communal/customary land remains a contested and difficult terrain for women to navigate. Whilst customary law allowed and continues to allow a woman to stay on the family communal land after the death of her husband, it is more difficult for the woman to stay on the same piece of land in the event of divorce. This is because communal land is considered as clan land, and therefore belonging to a man and his kinsmen. Since divorce is considered as a severance of the marriage relationship, not only between the woman and her husband, but also between the woman and the man's relatives, it is considered to be inconceivable that the women would be able to stay amongst the man's relative after a divorce (Mushunje, 2001:unpaginated) The result has been displacement of women from communal land after divorce, even in situations where the communal land is their only means of livelihood and regardless of their level of contribution towards the development of the communal land and attendant infrastructure.

In the event of a husband's death, a widow also faces challenges in maintaining her grip on the customary land as she faces hostilities and in some cases, land grabbing. It is almost impossible for a woman to remarry and continue occupying the land that she was occupying with the deceased husband. For example in 2021, two brothers from Manicaland were arrested for assaulting their widowed sister in law because she had remarried but continued to stay on the customary land that she used to occupy with her deceased husband.[14] Such hostilities and attitudes from families and communities are borne out of a belief that customary land belongs to the husband and his family or clan and as such a woman has no rights over such land.

2.4 Post-Independence Legislation Addressing Gender Inequality

The Legal Age of Majority Act, 1982 was the first attempt by the post-independence government to recognise the rights of women to be treated

---

14 Ncube L (2021) 'Two Possessive Siblings Jailed After Bashing Late Brother's Wife For Remarrying' available at: https://iharare.com/two-possessive-siblings-jailed-after-bashing-late-brothers-wife-for-remarrying/ (last accessed 28 February 2021)

as equals. However, as shown earlier, this Act was met with resistance even in the country's highest court through the *Magaya v Magaya* case.

Legislation recognising women's land rights was long in coming, seen as it was only promulgated in 2005 through section 23 (a) of the Constitution. This was an important provision in light of the country's land reform programme which began in 2000. This, however, was implemented in terms of the country's general laws and related only to agricultural land acquired by government from the former white commercial farmers. As such, challenges remained with regards to women's rights to customary land and their rights at customary law generally. This was because the general provision which allowed for discrimination against women on the basis of customary law and personal law in all other aspects of their lives still remained in the Constitution. As a result, the requirement not to discriminate against women on the basis of personal or customary law only in relation to accessing fast track land did not address the structural legal challenges that led to the perpetuation of discrimination against women in all other spheres of life. This gave the impression that this new provision with regards to access to fast track land for women was half-hearted, an add-on and a mere concession by government to pacify women in response to their demands for land. This did not help in changing the social perceptions with regards to women's rights but actually perpetuated the negative perceptions.

This masked the continuity in practice due to the perception that custom, customary law and patriarchy were not ready to fully embrace the rights of women. The refusal by government at this stage to totally outlaw discrimination emphasised the fact that customary law is a social and legal construction and its implementation is dependent on who in society has the power to design, interpret and implement it. Just as the colonial government pushed for the subjugation of women by arguing that providing for women's rights would anger the men in society and cause political turmoil, the post-independence government similarly feared that such provisions would not only alienate men generally but also traditional leaders and other male authorities such as church leaders. Their fear was that this could potentially cost them votes and political power.

For example in 1998 when the late Vice President, Joseph Msika, was a senior minister responsible for resettlement, he was quoted as insisting that government would not follow a policy of joint registration of land for married couples and would not prioritise single women and women heads of households in land allocations. His argument was that such an approach would give women too much freedom, was anti-culture and would invite the wrath of Zimbabwean men against the government.[15] The same perceived fears that the colonial government had of African men if African women were not 'controlled', were being projected by a post-independence black majority government. The concession in relation to non-discrimination in land reform and access to land by women in the 2005 constitutional amendment was in essence made so as not to totally 'rock the boat' but provide a bare minimum in order to address women's demands. The women had used their 'power with' to engage with visible power and demand their land rights. However, this was met with invisible power which stoked perceived customary and traditional practices to suppress the rights of women. To its credit, the 2013 Constitution expressly provides for women's rights to agricultural land whilst expressly outlawing discrimination on the basis of customary law. It also expressly provides for gender equality and gender balance in relation to access to land.[16]

The International Labour Organisation (ILO) has defined gender equality thus:

> …gender equality, or equality between men and women, entails the concept that all human beings, both men and women, are free to develop their personal abilities and make choices without the limitations set by stereotypes, rigid gender roles and prejudices. Gender equality means that the different behaviour, aspirations and needs of women and men are considered and valued and favoured equally. It does not mean that women and men have to become the same, but that their rights, responsibilities and opportunities will not depend on whether they are born male or female (ILO, 2000:48)

As such, gender equality between men and women in the context of the FTLRP implies equal treatment in accessing land regardless of sex or gender. The 2013 Constitution in demonstrating what gender balance should look like states in Section 17 (1) (b) that:

> The State must take all measures, including legislative measures,

---
15 *Irin News Africa*, 4 December 2002.
16 Sec 17, 56 and 289.

needed to ensure that:

i. both genders are equally represented in all institutions and agencies of government at every level; and

ii. women constitute at least half the membership of all Commissions and other elective and appointed governmental bodies established by or under this Constitution or any Act of Parliament.

Whilst this provision relates to gender balance in representation, the key concept to be gleaned is that gender balance entails equality or parity in numbers between men and women, boys and girls in the allocation of positions or in access to resources. In essence this would mean that access to A1 and A2[17] land by women and men in the country has an allocation rate of 50% for each gender.

The constitutional provisions referred to above were supported by the creation of constitutional institutions to ensure their implementation. Amongst these are the Zimbabwe Gender Commission (ZGC) and the Zimbabwe Land Commission (ZLC).[18] The ZGC is established specifically to monitor and ensure gender equality[19] and a key function of the ZLC is the elimination of gender discrimination in access, holding and occupation of land.[20] Put together, these and other institutions promoting democracy and human rights can be a force for positive change in promoting women's land rights in the country.

The post-independence legislative framework has therefore morphed from a generally repressive one for women, to one that seeks to protect women's rights, including rights of access to land. The promulgation of the 2013 Constitution, in particular, has marked a turning point from a legislative perspective. What remains is to ensure implementation of the Constitution, the creation of enabling legislation, and the harmonisation of laws to ensure the promotion of women's rights and gender equality..

---

17 The two main models that were used to affect the FTRLP were the small-scale A1 model (either as self-contained or villagised allocations) or the large-scale A2 model. However according to Scoones et al. (2011:2) 'in practice, the distinction between these models varies considerably, and there is much overlap'. In my study area, A1 allocations ranged in size from between 6-32 hectares and yet A2 farms in the sugar-cane estates in Chiredzi were as small as 18 hectares.

18 Provided for in Section 245 and Section 296 of the 2013 Constitution respectively.

19 Section 246 (a).

20 Constitution of Zimbabwe, 2013, Sec 297 (1) (c) (ii) (A).

2.5 Living Customary Law and Institutional Set-ups

Questions continue to be asked about whether adopting and promoting living customary law, which takes into account the lived realities and lives of communities, would be more useful than taking a legalistic approach and seeking to legislate acceptance of the rights of women by society. This is in line with the receptor approach which in relation to implementation of human rights obligations recognises that 'in Eastern and Southern states, international human rights obligations can be more fully implemented through local social institutions'. (Zwart, 2012:546). The receptor approach and the utility of living customary law will however need to be considered within the understanding that whilst flexible in some instances, in other instances communities' living customary law and local institutions can be more rigid and discriminatory towards women when compared to the state and the national courts' version of customary law (Hellum and Derman, 2013:158) and provisions of international human rights law.

The current practice by the Parliament of Zimbabwe to undertake public consultations in the law-making process as provided by the Constitution[21] is a recognition of the need to gather and understand public views and lived realities and incorporate these into the laws that Parliament eventually passes. Yet the living norms are shaped through power struggles as a result of the different views on what the law should be. Consultation can therefore lead to the projection and entrenchment of dominant views of the powerful, particularly men, who can easily access the spaces of power or platforms to contribute their views, whilst women are excluded through social, cultural, economic and other impediments. To address such challenges, the consultations must be undertaken with these disadvantages in mind, and should always be in accord with the constitutional imperatives of human rights, equality and non-discrimination.

In addition, the rights of women to land cannot rely entirely on the law but require the support of institutions and a positive infrastructure, without which the law is not easily implemented and women's rights to land fulfilled. Laws are a basic condition but on their own, they cannot

---

21 Constitution of Zimbabwe, Sec 141 (a) and (b) provides that Parliament must 'facilitate public involvement in its legislative and other processes and in the processes of its committees [and] ensure that interested parties are consulted about Bills being considered by Parliament, unless such consultation is inappropriate or impracticable'.

achieve the intended results. There is need, therefore, to ask whether such institutions and infrastructure were in place to aid in the FTLRP and protect the rights of women, and if not, how this impacted on women's chances of accessing land. Ikdahl, for example, argues that the political will to provide the necessary infrastructure is critical (Ikdahl, et al., 2005: xi) to ensuring access to land by women. In addition to enabling legislation, governments must put in place the conditions for women to participate in the land economy. This includes both the institutional and the physical infrastructure to facilitate such participation. For Zimbabwe's FTLRP this entailed the provision and decentralisation of government institutions such as the Ministry of Lands to assist and facilitate women's participation. It also meant the provision of physical infrastructure in the form of schools, water and health facilities, amongst others, to enable women to balance their productive and reproductive roles.

Many women from both communal and urban areas in my research area reported failure to participate in the FTLRP simply because the new farm areas were separate and distinct from their existing homes. For a long time, the new areas did not have the infrastructure for raising children and maintaining family relationships, given that the acquired commercial farms were vast tracts of land with centrally located and limited infrastructure The size of the white commercial farms before redistribution ranged from small holdings of 200 hectares to expansive land holdings of up to 10,000 hectares (Sarimana, 2005). As such, when the farms were divided up, access to buildings, farmworkers' houses, schools, clinics and dams amongst others was only for a very few of the people who were allocated land on the farms. The result was that women were forced to remain in their homes, whilst men went out in search of land and to camp on the inhospitable farms.

2.6 Role of Land Administration and Management Laws and Institutions

The Zimbabwe Land Commission is created under Section 296 of the Constitution with its key mandate being 'to ensure accountability, fairness and transparency in the administration of agricultural land that is vested in the State'.[22] This includes giving recommendations to government to ensure 'the elimination of all forms of unfair discrimination, particularly

---

22 Constitution, Section 297 (1) (a).

gender discrimination'.²³ Gender equality in access to land is a principle that ensures accountability, fairness and transparency in the management of agricultural land. It is therefore important that the ZLC is entrusted with the implementation of these tenets by the Constitution.

Given these constitutional provisions, this section will look at government's commitment to the ZLC and its mandate, and whether or not there has been any tangible efforts to ensure gender equality in access to agricultural land. Following its creation by the Constitution, the ZLC was established in 2016 when its Commissioners were sworn in by the President. The first Chairperson was a woman, a good signal in promoting gender equality and the equal participation of women at an institutional level as provided for in both the Constitution and the ZLC Act. The Commissioners²⁴ were however sworn in without an enabling Act of Parliament. This made it difficult for them to ensure effective mandate implementation. The Zimbabwe Land Commission Act: Chapter 20:29 was eventually promulgated in 2018. It played a role in promoting efforts towards the full operationalisation of the Commission. Most importantly, it provided for strong women's rights and gender equality provisions in relation to the allocation of, access to and control over state-owned agricultural land.

Section 36 (5) of the Act clearly states that applicable laws in relation to devolution of property upon marriage, the dissolution of marriage or death (amongst others) shall apply in relation to partially alienated state land,²⁵ unless another law specifically provides otherwise. This is a useful provision in light of interpretations which had been given by the courts until the promulgation of the Act.. The High Court in particular had concluded that fast track land is state land and thus cannot be subject to consideration in sharing of property at divorce as it does not form part of matrimonial property. Whilst the interpretations were gender neutral

---

23 Constitution, Section 297 (1) (c) (ii) (A).

24 The Commissioners were Mrs Tendai Bare (Chairpeson), Mr Tadious Muzoroza (Deputy Chairperson), Mr Abdul Gabriel Credit Nyathi, Ms Jeanatte Marrie Manjengwa, Ms Judith Buzuzi, Mr Emmanuel Eventhough Nyamusa, Ms Margaret Chinamhora, Mr Edmore Augustine Mugwagwa Ndudzo and Mr Luke Taurai Buka.

25 The Zimbabwe Land Commission Act Act does not define the terms 'partially alienated state land' but defines 'partially alienated state land rights' as a ninety-nine year lease or other lease of agricultural land; or a lease with a purchase option; or a permit; or an offer letter; and includes any right incidental to or connected with any of the foregoing Rights (Sec 2).

in that they allowed either of the spouses in whose name the lease was registered to retain the land upon divorce, substantively women suffered more from the negative effects of this interpretation given that most of the land acquired under the FTLRP was directly acquired by and registered in men's names. The cases of *Chiwenga v Chiwenga* and *Chombo v Chombo* referenced below were a clear example of how this interpretation by the courts disadvantaged women and their rights to agricultural land in the event of divorce. A Supreme Court Judgment following an appeal in the *Chombo v Chombo* case however overturned the High Court reasoning on sharing of fast track land rights upon divorce.[26]

Unlike the provisions of the Agricultural Land Settlement (Permit Terms and Conditions) Regulations, 2014 (S.I 53/2014) which recognise spouses of agricultural land holders (either as co-signatory permit holders or joint permit holders/joint heads of household)[27] the ZLC Act does not make similar provisions. Section 40 of the Act provides for the Register of Partially Alienated State Land Rights. In the register shall be entered the 'name of holder of every alienated State land right'.[28] The provision does not compel the registration of spouses as co-land rights holders or even just as spouses. Given that the Act was passed in 2018, four years after the promulgation of S.I 53/2014, it should have been expected that the Act would consolidate the positive provisions expounded in the Statutory Instrument and provide enhanced protections in that regard. Whilst marriage and other laws may be used to provide such protections in the event of death[29] or divorce, the mere act of registration of the rights of a spouse in the Register of Partially Alienated State Land was going to be an unambiguous means of recognising such rights in relation to agricultural land. It would also have been a demonstration of government efforts in institutionalising policy and legal coherence to ensure uniform implementation on the ground by the various actors and structures. Whilst in practice, the Ministry of Land, Land Reform and Resettlement requires all 99-year lease recipients to register their

---

26 This will be elaborated below.
27 Despite these positive provisions, I will explain later that even this S.I is flawed and does not fully protect the land rights of married women.
28 Zimbabwe Land Commission Act, Section 40 (2) (a).
29 As will be detailed later, when it comes to death, these provisions only apply in situations of intestate succession, and not testate succession as ruled by the Supreme Court in the case of *Chigwada v Chigwada* in December 2020.

spouses on the lease agreement, it remains necessary for such a provision to be legislated for in order to avoid discretional application of the policy position.[30] Compulsory joint registration would also be a positive step by government in demystifying the notion that land belongs to men, in particular the large-scale commercial farming land that is governed by the 99-year leases.

2.7 The Legal Framework for Land Audits

One of the major functions of the ZLC is 'to conduct periodical audits of agricultural land'.[31] The issue of identifying and documenting the access and control patterns following the FTLRP is vital for the government as well as for the people of Zimbabwe if the reform programme is to be considered a success by any standards or be put to rest. As the FTLRP unfolded, there were accusations that the programme benefitted mainly the elite and those with political connections (Bhatasara 2010: 28). Although government denied this, and insisted that the programme benefitted the landless majority, with over three hundred thousand (300,000) households having been allocated land, (Makwavarara et al. 2015) the fact that the elite and politically connected were given bigger and better pieces of land is undeniable (Bhatasara, 2010:28). In addition, the fact that this same elite acquired multiple farms or farms exceeding the maximum allowable hectarage is also a fact.[32] In February 2020, the Minister of Lands passed revised regulations on maximum farm sizes.[33] The regulations amended a 1999 Statutory Instrument (regulations) on farm sizes.[34] In terms of the 2020 regulations, the following are the maximum farm sizes for the different ecological regions of the country:

---

30 Interview with a Ministry of Lands Official on 1 July 2020.
31 Constitution of Zimbabwe, Section 297 (1) (b).
32 For example, after the deposition of former president Robert Mugabe, government acknowledged that he was a multiple farm owner.
33 Rural Land (Farm Sizes) (Amendment) Regulations, 2020 (No. 2) (SI 41 of 2020).
34 Rural Land (Farm Sizes) Regulations (SI 419 of 1999).

Natural Region[35]	Max Farm Size (in hectares)[36]
I	250 ha
II	500 ha
III	750 ha
IV	1,500 ha
V	2,000 ha

It is therefore imperative in terms of these regulations that land beneficiaries are not multiple land owners, and that their landholdings are within the legally set size limits. It is against this background that the ongoing land audits would assist the government in identifying those with multiple farms, or those whose farms exceed the maximum recommended farm sizes. In March 2020, the Minister of Lands reported that a second phase of the national agricultural land audit had been completed and the ZLC had submitted its audit report to the Minister.[37] The question that needs to be asked is how the land audit should help women to access more land under the FTLRP given that research conclusively shows that women did not benefit at the same level as men from the initial phases of the programme. Any land audit should not only seek to identify multiple land owners or those with farms that exceed the maximum farm size but must be used to address anomalies that existed from the onset of the programme. This will also help in creating good will from the citizens around the FTLRP and when used to increase access levels for women will ensure compliance with the Constitution which enjoins the government to ensure gender parity in all spheres of life.

---

35 These are agro-ecological regions, determined by soil type, vegetation and average annual rainfall. Region I is found in parts of the Manicaland Province with average annual rainfall of above 1000 millimetres whilst region II is found in parts of the three Mashonaland and Harare Provinces with annual average rainfall of between 700 and just above 1000 millimetres. Region III is found in parts of the Midlands, Mashonaland East, Mashonaland West, Manicaland, Masvingo, and Matabeleland North with average annual rainfall of between 500 and 700 millimetres. Region IV is found in all the provinces except for Harare with average annual rainfall of between 450 and 600 millimetres. Region V is found in parts of Masvingo, Matabeleland South, Matabeleland North, Midlands, Mashonaland West and Manicaland Provinces with average annual rainfall of below 500 millimetres (Source: Startupbiz, 'Natural Farming Regions in Zimbabwe' available at: https://startupbiz.co.zw/natural-farming-regions-in-zimbabwe/ (last accessed 20 November 2020).

36 Sec 3 (1).

37 *The Herald*, 12 March 2020.

The establishment of the ZLC and the enactment of the Zimbabwe Land Commission Act are milestones in in achieving this. The relatively high budgetary allocations to the ZLC (compared to other constitutional commissions, both independent and executive) is probably an indication of the government's commitment to ensuring that the ZLC is capacitated and in a position to fully implement its mandate and address the land question.[38]

Given that the fast track land audit issue has been long outstanding,[39] the ZLC must be assisted and capacitated to implement it.[40] The longer it takes to complete the audit and address any anomalies, the more likely it is that positions regarding allocations and access will become entrenched. Further delay will make it increasingly difficult to acquire any excess, underutilised or irregularly acquired land and redistribute it without causing major resistance and disruptions in future. Such entrenched positions are and will remain beneficial to men more than women in the country. In addition to entrenching existing control and access patterns over partially alienated state land, the delays in the land audit will also have the effect of cementing the widely held views that government is reluctant to undertake the audit because those who should be spearheading the process are multiple farm owners or possess land in excess of the required farms sizes and are therefore reluctant to implement the audit.[41] At a time when the post-Mugabe government is seeking re-engagement with the international community and seeking to open the country to foreign direct investment, addressing disparities in land ownership is an important way of attracting the necessary

---

38 At $10,49 million in 2019, the ZLC was given the highest budgetary allocation of all constitutional commissions in the country.

39 For example, as far back as 2009, the European Union was offering to assist government with the land audit but there was limited progress on the issue (See VOA, EU offers to fund Zimbabwe Land Audit – But Redistribution Hardliners Dig In. Available at: https://www.voazimbabwe.com/a/a-13-56-74-2009-10-09-voa53/1469338.html (last accessed 9 December 2020).

40 The ZLC Audit (or audits) would be one of many reports and audits that government has commissioned but whose recommendations it has failed, refused or neglected to implement. These include the outcomes of the Rukuni Commission (1994), the Utete Commission (2003), the Buka Land Audit (2003) and the Uchena Land Commission (2019).

41 David Smith (2010), 'Mugabe and allies own 40% of land seized from white farmers – inquiry' available at: https://www.theguardian.com/world/2010/nov/30/zimbabwe-mugabe-white-farmers (last accessed 9 December 2020).

support and goodwill. If, moreover, discrepancies in allocation are to be seriously addressed, they will necessarily have to take into account the gender-based disparities that continue to exist in land access, control and ownership patterns regarding the country's FTLRP. The land audit should be a priority mandate issue for the ZLC and the government in order to set the country on a path of gender equality in land access, ownership and control.

3

Women's Land Rights as a Human Right

3.1 Introduction

Specific land reform objectives may differ from country to country, but it is generally accepted that reform in any context is intended to address social, economic and political objectives (Gonese, et al., Undated:2). In some instances, land reform has signified or been accompanied by land law reform (Ikdahl, 2013) to inform and legitimise the process. At face value, Zimbabwe's land reform programmes have been premised on the need to address colonial historical imbalances and ensure that the country's disadvantaged population could benefit from the land. This might have been true of the country's initial land reform programme, implemented soon after independence and known as Land Reform and Resettlement Phase I. The view is, however, debatable, in relation to the FTLRP (also known as Land Reform Resettlement Phase II) given the manner in which the latter was implemented. Critics argue that the programme was primarily a reaction to the rejection in 2000 of a referendum of a government-led constitution, and the rising fortunes of a young opposition party, the Movement for Democratic Change (MDC) (Mutanda, D., 2013). They maintain that the FTLRP was an attempt to stop the new party in its tracks by using ZANU-PF's liberation war mantra of giving land to the majority blacks as a campaign theme (Human Rights Watch, Undated).

Other scholars argue that the major objectives of the land reform efforts were socio-political as the government sought to address the racial imbalances in land ownership (social objective) and ensure the fruits of the liberation struggle which was fought around the land question were realised (political objective). What eventually unfolded was a land reform programme that was premised on forcefully acquiring land from the white minority who were effectively being punished for supporting political opposition[1] and giving the land to the black majority. The racialised and highly politicised nature of the programme however meant that other forms of inherited legal disadvantage, including gender and age-based discrimination, and access to land were largely ignored in the implementation of both the first and second phases of the country's land reform programme. This chapter addresses the issue of whether or not the implementation modalities for the FTLRP addressed the issue of women's rights to agricultural land and the discrimination, long suffered, that women generally faced in relation to access to land, from colonial times.

3.2 Land Rights as a Women's Rights issue

Is there a right to land? This question has preoccupied researchers, human rights lawyers and human rights defenders. The debate arises from the fact that there is no right to land that is codified in international human rights law (Wickeri and Kalhan, Undated: 1). As such it would be a misnomer generally speaking to refer to women's rights to land, just as no other person is guaranteed a right to land in international law. Whilst land rights advocates may without hesitation insist that there is an international human right to land, some legal scholars argue that such a right does not exist because there are no international or regional treaties that expressly recognise a right to land. Provision on land rights mainly refer to rights to be treated equally in land reform, redistribution and access.[2]

Cordes however argues that even without an express right to land in international human rights law, a human right to land is emerging because 'human rights law is not static' (Cordes, 2017). She further argues that the international human right to land is emerging through advocacy by social movements engaging with visible power in both

---

1 The Human Rights Watch Report 'Land Reform in the Twenty Years After Independence' noted that 'the MDC was the first party to attract support from white Zimbabweans, and received significant financial support from the white business and commercial farming communities'.
2 For example, Article 14 (g) of CEDAW Provided for the rights of rural women to 'equal treatment in land and agrarian reform as well as in land resettlement schemes'.

national and international settings to ensure the recognition of such a right. Such engagements have influenced decisions and interpretations by international treaty bodies and tribunals who are increasingly reading the human right to land into international human rights treaties (Cordes, 2017).

In addition, the right to land in international law is also emerging through addressing the right to land in relation to specific interest groups. The Indigenous Peoples' rights movement for example has been built around the Indigenous Peoples' rights to land as recognised in international law. Part II of the ILO Indigenous and Tribal Peoples Convention, 1989 (No. 169) is dedicated to the right to land for Indigenous Peoples, with Article 14 providing that 'the rights of ownership and possession of the peoples concerned over the lands which they traditionally occupy shall be recognised' thereby providing an indisputable right to land. The United Nations Declaration on the Rights of Indigenous Peoples echoes similar provisions, stating that 'Indigenous peoples have the right to the lands, territories and resources which they have traditionally owned, occupied or otherwise used or acquired'.[3] Although the Declaration is not a binding instrument, the emphasis on the right to land for Indigenous Peoples is incontrovertible.

The protection of property rights as provided in international law and national constitutions is equally useful in arguing for the right to land, where the right is not specifically imbedded in national law. Various international human rights instruments make provision for this.[4] The Constitution of Zimbabwe also provides for property rights[5] and a specific right to agricultural land,[6] which places citizens, including women, on good grounds to claim the right. These provisions are essential in providing secure tenure to land, and the protection of women therein. Section 292 of the Constitution enjoins the government to take appropriate measures, including legislative measures to ensure security of tenure to any person owning or lawfully occupying agricultural land.

Derman and Hellum (2008), link land directly to the right to a

---

3   Article 26 (1).
4   For example, Article 17 of the Universal Declaration of Human Rights and Article 14 of the African Charter on Human and Peoples' Rights.
5   Section 71.
6   Section 72.

livelihood and the realisation that it is from land that many marginalised people, including women, rural communities and indigenous peoples derive their livelihoods. *The expectation, given the general movement toward giving legal recognition to the right to* land is that one of the key international treaty bodies will soon develop a general comment on the right to land, including the place of women therein, which can be used in the development of comprehensive international human rights instruments and national laws expressly providing for the right to land.

Without necessarily stretching the idea of having an explicit 'right to land' there are various international human rights instruments and principles as well as national laws that provide for 'land rights' and which can be effectively used to protect women in this regard. The FAO has developed various instruments that seek to strengthen access to land for the marginalised, including women, as a general human rights principle. The FAO Voluntary Guidelines on the Responsible Governance of Tenure of Land, Fisheries and Forests in the Context of National Food Security (2014) help in ensuring the recognition of women's land rights. The guidelines:

> Seek to improve governance of tenure of land, fisheries and forests… for the benefit of all, with an emphasis on vulnerable and marginalized people, with the goals of food security and progressive realization of the right to adequate food, poverty eradication, sustainable livelihoods, social stability, housing security, rural development, environmental protection and sustainable social and economic development (FAO Voluntary Guidelines 2014: 1).

Tied to this is the FAO technical guide for Governing Land for Women and Men (2013) which compliments the Voluntary Guidelines' principle of gender equality in tenure governance (FAO Governing Land for Women and Men, 2013:3). The technical guide addresses the need for national policies to identify and address issues that hinder gender equality in land access and control and attendant rights.

This emerging international policy framework can therefore be leveraged to grow and sustain current efforts to protect the land rights of women and other marginalised people and also seek the unequivocal recognition of the right to land in international and national law. The current framework also supports the link between land rights and various other rights that are expressly protected under international human rights law and whose enjoyment, realisation and fulfilment are directly correlated to land access, control and ownership. This can be used 'to facilitate the development of pro-poor and gender sensitive land policies [from a] human rights-based approach' (Ikdahl et al., 2005) with a realisation that developing strong land rights can be used as building blocks to advocate for an internationally recognised right to land.

3.3 The Link between Women's Right to Land and the enjoyment of other Rights

As shown above, there are various rights that can be derived by women in relation to land such as the right to equality[7] and therefore a right not to be discriminated against on the basis of gender or sex in land matters. In addition, it must also be realised that access to, ownership of and control over land directly impacts on other rights that are conferred on women in terms of international law. These include the right to food, housing, water, development, livelihood, and work amongst others. Land therefore plays a significant role in ensuring that these other rights as enshrined in national and international law are enjoyed and realised by women. The United Nations already acknowledges the link between access to land by women and their right to equality, to an adequate standard of living, to meeting their own needs and those of their families, global food security, sustainable economic development and even the fight against HIV and AIDS (United Nations, 2013). It also notes that land is not merely a commodity, but an essential element for the realisation of many other rights.[8]

As such, land can be looked at from various angles and contexts, including as an economic resource, a source of livelihood and a pointer to other basic rights. It can also be used as a measure of the application of the human rights principles of equality, equity and non-discrimination in relation to access to, control over and ownership of resources, particularly

---

7   For example, Article 14 (g) of CEDAW requires women to have 'equal treatment in land and agrarian reform as well as in land resettlement schemes'. This does not confer a right to land for women but a right to be treated equally in schemes addressing issues of access, ownership and control over land.

8   OHCHR, 'Land and Human Rights' available at: https://www.ohchr.org/EN/Issues/LandAndHR/Pages/LandandHumanRightsIndex.aspx (last accessed 20 November 2020)

between men and women. The result is that states have to regulate the competing needs for and demands over land in any setting and, in doing so, laws and law-making become necessary regulatory instruments.

International human rights frameworks often play a significant role in directing states in law-making by providing standards that are universally acceptable and applicable in relation to the protection and promotion of various rights. The FAO Guidelines, as stated above, are already guiding countries, including Zimbabwe in developing land law policies from a gender perspective. The African Union (AU) Framework and Guidelines on Land Policy in Africa offer an equally instructive tool. It recognises the impact of the patriarchal social organisation in impeding women's land rights and the need to dismantle, deconstruct, reconstruct and reconceptualise such land systems.[9] In a legal, social and economic system such as Zimbabwe's that has over time limited women's land rights on the basis of customary and cultural considerations, the AU Framework and Guidelines are instructive.

In the sections below, I provide an analysis of the right to water, to food and to a livelihood as examples of how these are linked to the right to land and the rights of women. The analysis recognises that there are many other rights that are linked to the right to land as elaborated above and therefore the focus on these three rights is not exhaustive. The focus on food, water and livelihood, however, seeks to illustrate their link with the right to land and to show why land is critical in the lives of women in Zimbabwe and throughout the world. This is framed in the bundle of rights framework, which defines the rights or streams of benefits that can arise from access to, ownership of and control over land. Using this framework, a determination can be made of 'different persons' legal title on the mineral, air, water, and/or surface rights associated with land at a particular location'.[10] The same framework can also be used to exclude the same persons from accessing other entitlements on the same piece of land such as minerals, oil and gas unless they obtain required permissions.[11] In all instances, access to, ownership of or control over the land helps in the determination of other rights and entitlements that are derived from

---

9   See Para 2.5.2: Land and gender relations.
10 Alan Schroeder (2001) 'Property and Property Rights' In *Property Rights: A Primer*. University of Idaho, College of Agricultural and Life Sciences, Bulletin 834 (revised).
11 Ibid.

the land. Access, control and ownership of land by women becomes an essential first step in ensuring a determination of the attendant bundle of rights, including the right to education, which can assist in giving women an alternative to working the land.

3.3.1 Land and the Right to Water

The focus on the right to land and water, as well as the right to land and food below is an acknowledgement of the indivisibility and interdependence of rights. Without access to land, particularly for women, it is difficult for them to enjoy other rights, including the right to water. The FAO notes that:

> In many jurisdictions, water rights have for a long time been considered as a subsidiary component of land tenure rights, a right to use water often being dependent on the existence of a land tenure right. (FAO, undated)[12]

In the past, the relationship between these two was tilted in favour of land rights, with a belief that access to water was often possible even in the absence of access to land. This may still hold true in many instances in contemporary societies, but the increasing pressure on water resources means that it will also become increasingly difficult to access water, without access to or control over land. The World Resources Institute (WRI) has noted that over a billion of the world's population live in water scarce regions and that by the year 2025, up to 3.5 billion people would be experiencing water scarcity (WRI, undated).[13] The result would be that those with control over the water will make it increasingly difficult for others to access the resource. Access to land will in such instances help in determining access to water, in relation to both physical water and underground water bodies. With limited access to land, women will bear the brunt of water access challenges, yet at the same time they will be expected to find and obtain water, especially for household and other primary uses, with a bearing on their and their families' livelihoods. In 2016, the United Nations Children's Fund (UNICEF) reported that women and girls worldwide spend 200 million hours every day collecting water and that this is a colossal waste of their valuable time (UNICEF, 2016) Thus, access to land for women is vital and their role in water

---

12 See http://www.fao.org/docrep/007/y5692e/y5692e02.htm
13 See https://www.wri.org/our-work/topics/water

resources management invaluable. Trivedi, 2018 notes that women's lack of involvement in the water sector is troubling not only for gender equity, but for peace and security as well. She also acknowledges the role that women play in water resources management by stating that 'women are the secret weapon for better water management' (Trivedi, 2018).

Clearly access to land by women not only enables their access to water but has also become a security issue given the emerging global challenges in relation to water. Lack of access to water for primary purposes has been defined as 'structural violence' in that it causes death through water-borne illnesses, especially amongst the under-fives, and leads to lost educational opportunities for girls who spend their time looking for water (as they do for wood fuel), and causes loss of agricultural productivity for rural women (Gehrig and Rogers, 2009).

In Zimbabwe's rural areas, gardening is a valuable contributor to household nutrition and reduced expenditure on food (Paradza, 2010). Furthermore, customary law recognises women's right to access land with available water in order to ensure family livelihoods. Hellum and Derman (2003) have pointed out that these customary practices can be compared to the human right to land and water. Access to the latter for irrigating gardens is critical to the success of gardening activities, freeing women and their families from water related 'structural violence' linked to malnutrition and lack of sustainable livelihoods. Access to water for such initiatives is in turn linked to women's access to land in their own individual right or as part of communities. Rutsate et al. explore customary norms that recognise the importance of vegetable gardens in the Mazowe District of Zimbabwe, noting that at customary law 'everyone had a right to have a garden by the river to meet families' nutritional needs' (2016: 434). This ensures access to both land and water. Using this norm, farmworker women in the district who had lost their jobs on large-scale commercial farms following the FTLRP ventured into adjacent communal land to establish vegetable gardens by the riverside as a form of livelihood. They faced no resistance from the area's traditional leader or other community members due to a recognition of their right to establish the gardens and using locally available water to irrigate them and sustain their livelihoods along the way.

Water has also been linked to the enjoyment of many other socio-economic rights. Hellum et al. (2016: 3) notes that:

from a gender perspective, the human right to water and sanitation is both a right in and of itself and a condition for the realization of other rights, most importantly the right to food, the right to health, the right to life, the right to a healthy environment, the right to education, the right to participation, and the right to gender equality.

They emphasise the importance of the indivisibility of socio-economic rights to poor and marginalised African women's right to adequate water for domestic and livelihood uses (Hellum et al., 2016:3). They also link Zimbabwe's Shona proverb 'water is life' to a broad right to livelihood for humans, animals and nature (Hellum et al., 2016:384). Whilst the Water Act [Chapter 20:24) recognises the right to access water for primary purposes,[14] it goes further to state that this provision 'shall not be construed as conferring on any person a right, which he [or she] would not otherwise possess, to enter or occupy any land for the purpose of abstracting the water'.[15] This links back to the centrality of land in order for one to access water, given that a person on whose land water is found, can deny access to other people. The 'water is life' proverb or customary norm, where it applies, becomes a fall-back position to ensure that people are guaranteed water for primary use purposes as a human right. This aligns with the view that state law is not the sole regulatory mechanism of people's access to water…women's right to water and participation in water governance [because it] is affected by legal pluralism i.e. the co-existing, overlapping, and sometimes conflicting, human rights and statutory law, as well as local norms and practices (Hellum et al., 2016:385). In situations where state law and failure to access land stifle these rights, customary norms in Zimbabwe can play a role in protecting and promoting women's right to water.

3.3.2 Land and the Right to Food

The right to food is linked to both the right to land and the right to water. Effectively, this is a strong indication of the indivisibility and interdependence of these rights and human rights generally. Given this

---

14 Primary purposes in relation to the use of water is defined in the Act as: reasonable use of water – for basic domestic human needs in or about the area of residential premises; or for the support of animal life, other than fish in fish farms or animals or poultry in feedlots; for the making of bricks for the private use of the owner, lessee or occupier of the land concerned; or for dip tanks;

15 Sec 32 (1).

realisation, the right to food and water are set out and combined in one section in the 2013 Constitution, Section 77. This states that every person has a right to 'safe, clean and potable water' and 'sufficient food' with the state being obliged to ensure that it takes 'reasonable and other legislative measures within the limits of the resources available to it, to achieve the progressive realisation of this right'.[16] The wording in this section of the Constitution actually shows that the right to water and food is treated as one right and not two different rights. Invariably it means that it is impossible to enjoy one without the other, at least when linking the right to potable water with the right to food. The enjoyment of both rights, especially for rural women is closely linked to the right to land. The Global Water Partnership (GWP) notes that 'food production principally depends on the availability of fresh water and arable land' (GWP, 2014:4). They argue further that:

> Land tenure and use practices can significantly influence water availability and quality and, in turn, water availability and quality affect how we use land to produce food (GBW, 2014:4).

This statement stresses the need to protect the various rights in order to ensure an adequate standard of living for citizens. States are therefore obliged to ensure that the interlinking nature of the rights is fully recognised in order for these rights to be fully realised by the citizens. Given the challenges that women face in accessing their rights of ownership, control and access to land, deliberate efforts need to be made to ensure protection, especially where such access is impacted on by unequal access and gender-based discrimination in access to land.

Research by the United Nations Human Rights Council Advisory Committee on Rural Women and the Right to Food concluded that in order for women to enjoy their right to food, they should have access to income-generating resources such as land and enjoy inheritance rights amongst other necessities. They concluded that any exclusions or restrictions based on gender and suffered by rural women in their efforts to access essential resources violate this right (UN Human Rights Council 2012:5). In such instances, state parties have an obligation to enact laws that ensure property and inheritance rights, including those of land in order for women to enjoy their right to food. The UN Special Rapporteur

---

16 Constitution of Zimbabwe, section 77.

on the Right to Food has also emphasised the need for gender-sensitive agricultural policies that ensure women's full participation in the economy and women's right to inherit and possess land and access other productive resources (UN Human Rights Council, Special Rapporteur on the Right to Food, 2012:14). Noting the key role played by land in ensuring food security for women, the Special Rapporteur noted that:

> Land is more than an economic asset that women should be allowed to use productively. It is also a means of empowerment, as the greater economic independence that results from land ownership enhances the woman's role in decision-making and allows her to garner more social, family and community support (UN Human Rights Council, Special Rapporteur on the Right to Food, 2012:16).

Article 14 of CEDAW on rural women and their right to access land, water, development infrastructure and related rights is premised on the recognition that rural women are disadvantaged partly because they are women and partly because they are rural. Hellum in this regard notes that:

> Although the Women's Convention does not explicitly refer to intersectional discrimination suffered by women by virtue of their sex and other status, it recognises that different groups of women such as… rural women… may be subject to intersectional discrimination based on both their sex and other characteristics (2013:613).

In addition, the CEDAW Committee in General Recommendation Number 28 Para 18 also flagged the importance of intersectionality as a basic concept in understanding the scope of obligations of State Parties in relation to the elimination of all forms of discrimination against women as contained in Article 2 of the Convention. This entails an understanding of the fact that:

> Discrimination of women based on sex and gender is inextricably linked with other factors that affect women, such as race, ethnicity, religion or belief, health, status, age, class, caste, and sexual orientation and gender identity (Para 1).

Rural women in particular often face the challenges of discrimination as women and on the basis of these other grounds in relation to access to land, and ultimately in enjoying the right to food. This calls for special attention by governments in land reform by ensuring that rural women are properly recognised in land allocation. Looking at the initial land reform planning soon after independence both women and rural populations were supposed to become beneficiaries of land reform. The Implementation Plan prioritised the following categories of people:

- Landless people/families
- Unemployed and poor families prepared to relinquish all land rights in communal areas
- Returning war of liberation refugees
- Experienced communal farmers prepared to relinquish all land rights in the communal areas
- Communal farmers with master farmer certificates
- Single women (widowed and divorced)

(*Source*: Zimbabwe Land Reform and Resettlement Programme: Phase I, 1980-1997)

The communal (rural) farmer and single women were clearly identified as requiring prioritisation in land allocation. There was, however, failure to intersect the communal (rural) aspects with the women's rights issues in order to address the intersectional discrimination that rural women, including married women, face in relation to access to land, and ultimately their right to food. Understanding and addressing such intricacies would go a long way in addressing the rights of rural and other deserving women to land so that they could enjoy their right to food. The focus of Phase I of the Land Reform and Resettlement Programme on single women and the assumption that married women would benefit from land reform through their husbands only offered a simplistic approach that failed to take into consideration the intersectional discrimination that women face, and the fact that loss of land led to food insecurity. Effectively at dissolution of marriage, the women who benefitted from land through their husbands under the programme lost not only the land, but were exposed to food insecurity as well.

3.3.3 Land and the Right to a Livelihood

The 2013 Constitution enjoins the state and all its institutions 'to provide everyone with an opportunity to work in a freely chosen activity, in order to secure a decent living for themselves and their families'.[17] For many women in Zimbabwe, this is closely tied to land, as it is the primary asset for the enjoyment of that right. This applies to land held or accessed under different tenure systems such as communal land and fast track land.

Women in rural areas often grow food for basic family food needs. However, even those who farm at a subsistence level, often have surplus to sell, and use the proceeds for other needs such as healthcare, education and clothing amongst others. For women who farm at a commercial level, land forms the basis of their incomes and the attendant needs and livelihoods for their families.[18]

The right to livelihood has also been linked to the right to dignity, a fundamental right that any human being is entitled to. The Constitution of Zimbabwe provides for the right to dignity and further states that 'no law may limit… the human right to dignity'[19] an indication of its overarching position. This provision is in line with the Universal Declaration of Human Rights, which states that 'all human beings are born free and equal in dignity and rights'.[20] Denying women access, control and ownership of land directly impacts their rights to a livelihood and in turn their right to human dignity. The FAO makes a clear link between access to land and a life with dignity for women by ensuring an adequate standard of living, economic independence and personal empowerment.[21] This in turn has implications for women's personal security, protection from gender-based violence, including domestic violence in situations where they are forced to live in abusive relationship because of lack of alternative accommodation and means of livelihood. A right to land and the attendant right to livelihood ultimately defines the humanity of many of Zimbabwe's women.

---

17 Constitution of Zimbabwe, 2013, sec 24 (1).
18 The 2017 National Gender Profile of Agriculture and Rural Livelihoods estimated that following land redistribution, women had 36.6% of small scale commercial land and 19.4% of large scale commercial land.
19 Constitution of Zimbabwe, 2013, sec 86 (3) (b).
20 Article 1.
21 FAO (2010). Land and Property Rights: Junior Farmer Field and Life School – Facilitator's Guide. Rome.

4

Impact of Violence on Women's Rights to Access Land under the Fast Track Land Reform Programme

4.1 Introduction

Given that I consider the FTLRP as a framework of analysis, it is necessary to examine some of the key characteristics of the programme and how these impacted women's right to access land on the basis of equality with men. One of the uncontested characteristics of the FTLRP was the violence that accompanied it, particularly during the early stages of the programme (UNDP, 2002:35). This was meted out against the white commercial farmers, their farmworkers and anyone who was deemed opposed to the violent take-over of the farms or the initiative in general. The UNDP noted in relation to farmworkers that:

> The violence to which many farm workers have been exposed since early 2000, together with increasing uncertainty about their future and their ability to sustain access to basic education and health services for their families, has led to heightened levels of depression and despair among many of them (UNDP, 2002:35).

The violence against this subgroup was pervasive and had impacts that went beyond the immediate issue of farm occupations, dispossessions and evictions. It impacted the farmworkers' livelihoods, health and the educational needs of their children. As will be elaborated below, my field research showed that violence was prevalent amongst the perpetrators of the farm occupations and invasions as well. Farm owners also bore the brunt of the violence, with Eddie Cross[1] indicating that up to 28 farmers[2] were killed between 2000 and 2014 and 'that 78 black Zimbabweans who were farm managers were also murdered during this period' (Cross, 2017:unpaginated).[3] Other farmers and farmworkers were injured and had their homes burnt or destroyed. In such an environment, how were Zimbabwean women supposed to benefit from the land?

In General Recommendation Number 19,[4] the CEDAW Committee recognised violence as a form of discrimination that seriously inhibits women from enjoying their rights and freedoms. This is particularly the case when the violence is directed at women *per se* or when it disproportionately affects women when compared to men. The consequences of violence generally and violence against women specifically are that it maintains women in subordinate positions, limits their participation in political and public life and in the attainment of work and access to resources.[5] The violence that women experience can be both interpersonal and structural. Often, it is the latter that leads to the perpetuation of interpersonal violence against women.

In defining structural violence, Galtung has argued that:

> There may not be any person who directly harms another person in the structure. The violence is built into the structure and shows up as unequal power and consequently as unequal life chances. Resources are unequally distributed… Above all, the power to decide over the distribution of resources is unevenly distributed (Galtung, 1969:171)

---

1   Mr Eddie Cross was the former MDC Member of Parliament for Bulawayo South and current (2020) member of the Reserve Bank of Zimbabwe Monetary Policy Committee (MPC).

2   The number is higher than what is normally reported, with some reports giving figures ranging from seven (Human Rights Watch) to twelve (see https://www.news24.com/news24/Africa/Zimbabwe/white-farmers-killers-should-not-be-prosecuted-mugabe-declares-20170815 (last accessed 26 February 2021). In his report, Mr Cross however provides a list of names, and the dates of the murders, pointing to the accuracy of the figures. The difference in numbers could also be attributed to the fact that the smaller numbers related to the earlier years of the programme, whilst Mr Cross' count spans 14 years.

3   Available at: http://www.eddiecross.africanherd.com/170816.html (last accessed 26 February 2021)

4   11th Session, 1992.

5   CEDAW Committee General Recommendation Number 19, on Violence Against Women, Para 11).

An ingrained feature of structural violence against women is its ability to deny them access to resources including land due to unequal power relations. Such a structure usually favours men who have access to resources and the power to distribute them, more and better education, political influence and general control over institutions and processes. Women by comparison are dependent, have little bargaining power and are thus vulnerable to violence and abuse. In such situations 'power over' is used to keep women down and to emphasise their weak positions within different social gradients within families, communities (such as local/farm levels) and society at large (at the national level).

Structural violence often leads to interpersonal violence where physical force is used on women because of their vulnerability. The World Health Organisation (WHO) defines interpersonal violence as:

> The intentional use of physical force or power, threatened or actual, against oneself, another person, or against a group or community, that either results in or has a high likelihood of resulting in injury, death, psychological harm, mal-development or deprivation (Krug, et al., 2002:5).

The end result is that women who are on the receiving end of violence are unable to participate in economic activities that should otherwise enable them to prosper and break the cycle of poverty and violence. Fear and embedded bottlenecks (invisible power) result from the existence of structural violence whilst fear and violence related pathologies are a real impediment to participation in the economy and society, in particular in situations where physical violence is employed. It is in this context that the violence that accompanied the initial stages of the FTLRP in Zimbabwe must be analysed, especially bearing in mind that the violence was a perpetuation of a culture that dated back to the country's liberation struggle which was fought between 1966 and 1979. The violence against women during this period was physical, sexual and even emotional. Chogududza (Undated:18) notes that:

> An examination of internal ZANU documents and interviews with female ex-combatants reveal that sexual abuse of women fighters by male guerrillas was rampant with perpetrators ranging from the lowest ranks to the highest leadership. Reports indicate that senior officers in the camps forced themselves upon young female

combatants, black and white soldiers on their female victims, while guerrillas demanded sexual gratification from their female counterparts.

Women therefore suffered sexual and other violence from all sides of the conflict with the guerrilla fighters for example using the night vigils (*pungwes*) as opportunities to sexually assault women and young girls (Chogugudza, Undated:18). Female freedom fighters such as Margaret Dongo, Oppah Muchinguri, Fay Chung and Freedom Nyamubaya[6] have been at the forefront of highlighting the violence and abuse that women suffered during the liberation struggle, although by and large, these atrocities have been hushed up by the country's leaders.[7] In 2016, the *Zimbabwe Independent*, a weekly newspaper, carried a story in which one commentator lamented that:

> It's sad that the suffering of female combatants during the war has hardly received official recognition by the government, 36 years after the war ended. Female fighters endured not only the trauma of war, but also carried the added burden of being sexually abused by some of their own comrades and commanders, a number of whom may still occupy positions of leadership and authority in the government and state institutions.[8]

The result has been unhealed wounds on the part of both freedom fighters and civilian women[9] who bore the brunt of the violence and a default to violence by the country's men, both former freedoms fighters and civilians whenever there is a disagreement. Violence during the FTLRP and the minimisation of women's contribution during the programme, was in essence a reiteration of the lived experiences of women during the country's liberation struggle. This effectively limited women's participation in the FTLRP as land beneficiaries for fear of physical/interpersonal violence while the implicit structural violence, even where

---

6   All of them are either well-known female leaders or women's rights, gender and human rights activists and defenders in the country.
7   'Sexual Abuse: The Untold Story of the Liberation War' (*The Independent*, Harare, 26 August 2016) available at: https://www.theindependent.co.zw/2016/08/26/sexual-abuse-untold-story-liberation-war/ (last accessed 16 May 2020)
8   Ibid
9   Civilian women who remained behind serviced the freedom fighters with food, clothes, and other necessities also sacrificed their children who went to join the struggle.

no direct violence was applied or implied against them was ever present. The FTLRP was invariably referred to as *jambanja*[10] by Zimbabweans, a term that has come to signify strife and violent situations. Below I elaborate the role of the different actors or perpetrators of violence and the different violent actions, those who were on the receiving end and how these impacted women's ability to access land as equals to their male counterparts.

4.2 The War Veterans of Zimbabwe's War of Independence

The veterans of Zimbabwe's war of liberation were central protagonists in the farm invasions and the FTLRP generally and not for the first time. They have been a constant presence in many contentious, rebellious and violent events post-1980. They have displayed both their 'power with' through collective actions and their 'power over' by instilling fear in other citizens. Occasionally, they even showed their ability to challenge government on a number of issues including its alleged failure to give them due recognition for their role in the war of liberation. For example, their protests and threats in 1997 culminated in the government's capitulation when President Mugabe agreed to give the war veterans a Z$50,000[11] lump-sum payment (gratuity) for their role in the liberation struggle, despite the negative impact that this unbudgeted payment would have on the country's economy. The government gave in so as to avoid a protracted, potentially politically ruinous confrontation with the war veterans and their 'power with'. The shock to the economy caused by these payments plus factors such as the country's participation in the Democratic Republic of Congo war in 1998, triggered the beginning of hyperinflation in the country (Munangagwa, 2009:121). The war veterans' success in this endeavour was succeeded by various other confrontations as provided below and each success provided them with the impetus to make larger demands, including those for land as they realised that their threats could produce results. The use of violence, coercion and other forms of 'mobilisation' by the war veterans to get their way during the land reform programme and in other antagonistic situations in Zimbabwe is well documented

---

10 IGI Global defines the term jambanja as 'A Shona neologism that refers to the forced takeover of white commercial farms by indigenous blacks under the so-called fast-track land reform program (FTLRP)'.
11 About US$4,000 at the time

(Sadomba, 2008, Horace, 2003, Raftopoulos and Savage (eds), 2004). Sadomba and Andrew describe this situation thus:

> The war veterans' movement first engaged the State in a 'no-holds-barred' meeting on 25 April 1992, making their demands to President Mugabe. With Chenjerai Hunzvi at the helm of the [Zimbabwe National Liberation War Veterans Association] ZNLWVA, their strategy became more militant and included direct confrontations. They organised street demonstrations, locked Ministers and top ZANU (PF) politicians in their offices, disturbed an international conference and a Heroes' Day speech by Mugabe, interrupted court sessions and besieged the State House. (Sadomba and Andrew, 2006:9)

Their approach, whenever they felt that their issues were not being addressed, was militant, and often the militancy bordered on or was effectively violent, thereby impacting on the rights of others.

Despite receiving the gratuity in 1997, the war veterans continued to make demands, this time insisting that they wanted to be allocated land, as it was one of the primary reasons the country fought for liberation. Being the main protagonists of the war of liberation, arguably the war veterans had a right to make this demand and but for the attendant violence, this was, in my view, a noble call. The President and Government of Zimbabwe yielded to the War Veterans demands and promised them 20% of all land to be redistributed under the FTLRP (Sadomba and Andrew, 2006:9). As Table 4.1 shows, the 20% figure was surpassed and the war veterans got 27% of all the land that was distributed under the FTLRP.

Table 4.1: Land Reform Beneficiaries by 2013

Beneficiaries (households)	A1	A2	Total
War veterans	32,550	3,793	36,343
Women	13,020	1,517	14,537
Youths	651	76	727
Mixed beneficiaries[12]	116,529	13,580	130,109

Source: Table adapted from the ZANU (PF) 2013 Election Manifesto (Page 57)[13]

---

12 The statistics would have been more useful with a further disaggregation of these mixed beneficiaries.

13 These statistics must be read sceptically considering that they were presented by

I used Gaventa's power cube[14] as an analytical framework for assessing the dimensions and typologies of power as well as the levels, nature and forms of power relationships, spaces for engagement and the actors that the war veterans had to engage with in order to access land. I concluded that their success could be attributed to the ability to deploy their 'power with' and mobilise as war veterans to confront visible state power at the national level. The militant nature with which they confronted visible power showed that their collective resolve had the capacity to effectively challenge state power and threaten the continued existence of the government of the day. The state was, therefore, left with no choice but to yield to the demands of the war veterans and give them the land.

In February of 2000, war veterans launched attention grabbing farm occupations in the country's Masvingo Province. They had over the years propounded a clear position on land, which focused on large-scale expropriation of white land without compensation (Matondi, 2012:21). They were therefore often viewed as the *de facto* leaders of the farm invasions, land allocation and redistribution and the champions of the land reform programme in the country.

The war veterans' power and authority was evident in both A1 (Chidza Farm, Lothian Farm and Masimbiti in Nuanetsi Ranch) and the A2 (Hippo Valley Estates, Farm 54 and Musisinyani area) in my research area as they were key in co-ordinating the farm invasions and the initial settlement following the invasions. The A1 farms were small-scale farms, some in villagised models whilst others were self-contained. The sizes of an A1 farm in my research area ranged between 6 hectares (Masimbiti in Nuanetsi Ranch) and 32 hectares (Lothian Farm in Masvingo District), and everything in-between. The A2 allocations were generally viewed as commercial in their operations but with varying sizes. The A2 farms that were the subject of my research in Hippo Valley were small scale in operation and small in size as well, with some as small as 18 or 20 hectares. Their distinguishing factor from the A1 farms was not necessarily the size but the nature of the farming operations taking place on the land. The A2 farms in Hippo Valley were regarded as such (commercial) because they

---

ZANU-PF, a party that rode on the 'successes' of the land reform programme as an election rallying point. The point to be stressed from the statistics is the skewed access levels for women when compared with other social groups that are highlighted in the Table.

14 As detailed in Chapter 1.

were farms on which farmers grew sugar-cane on a commercial basis.

During the early stages of the farm invasions and occupations, the war veterans often unilaterally created rules that everyone on the farm was expected to abide by. They were generally accepted as the leaders of the land invasions process, showing their 'power over' the other protagonists at the local/farm level. To sustain support for the farm invasions, the war veterans used violence, intimidation, political rhetoric and often whipped up emotions through the invocation of the memories of both the first and second Chimurenga,[15] the relationship between land and traditional religion, i.e. the need to appease the spirits of the ancestors and the departed war comrades. Mr FZ[16] one of the key war veteran leaders at Lothian Farm had this to say:

> We had to teach people about the history of Zimbabwe and the war of liberation. This helped them to understand the importance of the land reform programme as the war was fought in order for us to get the land. These teachings were given during meetings to discuss land allocations, to plan our future on the farms but also during the *pungwes* (all night vigils) at the farms.[17]

Mr FZ emphasised that the spirits of the war dead would not rest until the war of liberation had been taken to its logical conclusion through the return of land to the black majority. This invisible form of power influenced him and others in their approach to the land question. My interactions with him showed that war veterans developed institutions that were modelled along wartime institutions, in particular the bases, which were headed by the war veterans themselves as base commanders. Mr FZ was the base commander at Lothian Farm at the time of the farm invasions although he had relinquished that position with the coming in of new institutional structures on the farm as government moved in to rationalise and properly allocate the invaded land.[18]

The wartime institutions that were established at the beginning of

---

15 These were Zimbabwe's wars of liberation from colonial rule. The first Chimurenga was fought between 1896 and 1897, only a few years after colonial settlement. The Africans were defeated by the colonial settlers in this war. The Second Chimurenga, which led to the independence of the country from colonial rule in 1980, was fought between 1966 and 1979.
16 Mr FZ died on 18 October 2016.
17 Interview with Mr FZ in Masvingo on 10 February 2012.
18 Government created the Committees of Seven and even Village Heads on the farms.

the farm invasions were still evident in Nuanetsi Ranch's Masimbiti area/Ward 16, as the area had not yet been pegged and reallocated by government. The settlers in this area portrayed the 'base commander' of Kugarahunzwanana Village in Ward 16, Mr OC as a strongman. The settlers were reluctant to discuss the land issue with me before obtaining his approval. When I eventually spoke to him he gave a narrative of his role during the farm invasions, in particular the fact that it was he and a few other men, mostly war veterans, who led the invasion of the area. He indicated that when the other people came in to join them, they had already put rules in place on how the land invasion and allocation process was to be governed. The 'newcomers' therefore had to abide by those rules. He emphasised that this was necessary in order to ensure 'order and discipline' so that the land reform programme would not be derailed but be seen through to its logical conclusion.[19]

The findings in this instance correlated with those of other researchers on the violent role of the war veterans in the land reform programme and in other political and social settings in the country. Given that it was the male war veterans in particular who led the violent invasions and set the rules of engagement on the occupied farms, those who attempted to join the process late, the majority of whom were women, were either forced to live by the rules, or leave the farms and forget about acquiring land.

The development of wartime institutions and the rise of the war veterans as the *de facto* leaders of the farm invasions and land allocations gave them incredible power and authority which were seldom questioned by the other farm invaders. This was despite the disquiet about the manner in which they were directing the processes on the farms. Whilst the war veterans viewed their iron grip on the process as necessary in order to instil 'order and discipline', the other settlers viewed the rules as oppressive and unfair, although they could not say it openly. One of my respondents, Mrs MN was one of the few early women land invaders on Nuanetsi Ranch.[20] By the time I spoke to her, she had retreated to her rural home in the adjacent Musvovi Communal Lands because she

---

19 During interviews with the settlers and MR OC on 22 April 2011.
20 The Ranch is located in Mwenezi District, Masvingo Province. At close to 1 million hectares in size, it occupies nearly 1% of Zimbabwe's land size is considered the largest privately owned conservancy in Africa (See 'Nuanetsi: A case of wasted investment, stolen livelihoods', available at: https://www.zimbabwesituation.com/news/nuanetsi-a-case-of-wasted-investment-stolen-livelihoods/)

found the violence, threats and the general environment on the ranch untenable. She told me that:

> The war veterans were the ones who controlled the process and many people complained that it was not being done properly and that the war veterans were abusing people and forcing them to do things that they did not want to do. At one time we were forced to go and block the main Ngundu-Chiredzi Road[21] at Masimbiti. We were even told that we were supposed to dig up the tarred road so as to prevent the white farmers from accessing their farms.[22] We were told that this was a war and that we had to do those things if we were to win the war. They said if you did not participate in the 'war', then you would not get the land.[23]

The Nuanetsi Ranch allocation was an A1 allocation but women in A2 allocations confirmed having similar experiences. Mrs C whose allocation was in the A2 sugar-cane plantations in the Musisinyani area of Hippo Valley spoke of how war veteran leaders forced farm invaders to stay on the farms to keep the numbers of farm invaders high.[24] This was done to give the impression that there were 'multitudes' of people in need of land as demonstrated by their camping on the farms. Mrs MN, from Musvovi Communal lands, quoted above, also reported that war veteran leaders stopped farm invaders from visiting their pre-existing rural homes without permission and beyond the number of days allocated to visit the rural areas (at most two days). She said the war veteran leaders argued that if people stayed away from the farms for long periods, this would deplete the numbers of people camping on the farms and give the impression that the farm invasions were not popular. She reported that the war veterans assumed unquestionable power (power over) and one was either forced to accept their leadership and instructions if they wanted land, or if they disagreed, to leave the farms and return to their original homes. She also complained that the war veterans used threats and intimidation to

---

21 The Ngundu-Chiredzi Road is a national highway that links the country's sugar producing district of Chiredzi with the rest of the country and in particular with Masvingo, Harare, Bulawayo and the Beitbridge border with South Africa.
22 The settlers did not however dig up the road, showing that this was mere rhetoric on the part of the war veterans.
23 Interview with Mrs MN in the Musvovi Communal Lands in Masvingo District on 23 April 2011.
24 Interview with Mrs C on 10 February 2012 in Masvingo.

collect contributions in cash and kind for various 'projects' on the farms but such contributions were never properly accounted for. Such 'projects' they were told, included visiting government offices in Masvingo or Chiredzi to discuss the occupations or to bring officials to address the land occupants about their tenancy on the farms. However, because the war veterans were the authority on the farms, the people had to follow such instructions or risk losing out on land allocations.

The above narratives show that violence, coercion and intimidation were very much a part of the land reform process, were in many instances perpetrated by the male war veterans, and just as in the liberation struggle, women bore the brunt of the violence. As a result, some women abandoned their quest to acquire land under the FTLRP and retreated to their original homes. The effect of the violence was to discriminate against women who found themselves unable to participate in the FTLRP as a result. Nonetheless, some women managed to acquire land when the government introduced the land application process, following the invasions and started proper land allocations based on these applications as detailed below.

4.3 Land Applications, Rationalisation and Regularisation

After the initial chaos of land invasions, government moved in and started to put some rules in place. It encouraged people to apply for land in order for their applications to be assessed and decisions made about their eligibility to get land. The application process was particularly adhered to in relation to A2 allocations. According to a senior provincial official in the Ministry of Lands in Masvingo, after the initial land invasions:

> It became government policy that applications for A2 farms would be centralised and decided on at the provincial level[25] through the Provincial Lands Committee (PLC). The District Lands Committee (DCL) could identify suitable land and beneficiaries but the ultimate decision was made at the provincial level.

At this stage, women who had failed to acquire land during the violent

---

25 Mr DM, an official in the Masvingo Office of the Ministry of Lands and Rural Resettlement on 10 February 2012 stressed that 'The District Land Committee is responsible for recommending A2 farmers that can be allocated land but the actual allocation for A2 farms is carried out by the Provincial Lands Committee', confirmed this.

farm invasions were able to make applications and have their applications considered in an orderly manner. However, even with this approach, only women with certain knowledge, skills sets[26] and conversant with the process were able to engage with it, leaving out those, who however deserving, did not possess the requisite skills. A female respondent who applied for land in the Hippo Valley sugar-cane estates had this to say:

> I was staying in Chiredzi town at the beginning of the farm invasions.[27] I got an application form from a friend who encouraged me to apply for land when it was announced that people could apply for land in the sugar cane estates. I hand delivered my application form directly at the Masvingo Ministry of Lands and Rural Resettlement Provincial Offices. In 2001, when they announced that the successful names were out, I went to the [District Administrator] D.A's office in Chiredzi and my name was on the notice board as one of the successful applicants. By then the offer letter was already at the D.A's offices.[28]

The above respondent was well-educated and a business woman, running a number of grocer's shops in Masvingo Province. She was able to make the required application for a sugar-cane plot when the violence subsided and government restored order, thereby allowing people to participate in the process in an organised way. She used her education to compile the application for an A2 sugar-cane plot, which required completing a detailed application form and preparing a business plan as part of the application. She also needed to present a convincing argument to show that she could effectively utilise the farm by providing proof of financial resources, an acceptable level of education and experience in running a business. She also used the resources from her business including money and a motor vehicle to traverse the province, including travelling to the relevant district and provincial offices to submit her application and follow up on it. The 'power within' that she possessed was of immense value. These were not characteristics that could be associated with ordinary rural women in need of land.

The application approach was not widely used in relation to the A1 allocations, even after the initial violence had subsided. In these

---

26 For example, one needed to submit a business plan in order to access A2 land.
27 She, however, did not participate in the farm invasions.
28 Interview with Mrs AM in Hippo Valley (Farm 54) on 6 February 2012.

allocations, government moved in to regularise and rationalise the land allocations, based on who was already in occupation on the farms.[29] In many instances, government simply put in place systems to manage the land reform programme *ex post facto* of the invasions and self-settlement by people.

Researchers such as Matondi and Moyo have argued that a significant amount of land was acquired through proper applications for land to government, followed by allocation and settlement and not necessarily through invasions. However, in my research area, invasions and occupations were the underlying *modus operandi* in acquiring land in all the three locations that were the focus of my research, albeit with variations. In the Hippo Valley Estates (A2 allocation) for example, even after invading the farms, the invaders made formal applications for land whilst they camped on the farms. They also applied for some of the assets on the farms (in particular houses). These included the main farmhouses and the staff (compound) houses, which were allocated to the resettled farmers individually once they were given their portion of land on the farm. In the other two locations (Lothian/Chidza and Nuanetsi) no application process was required and settlers were allocated land by virtue of invasions and self-settlements. In terms of law-making, government promulgated the laws in retrospect as it struggled to manage the various facets of the land reform programme such as claims from the dispossessed farmers, ensuring security for the resettled farmers, with the aim of stabilising the process from a social, political and economic perspective.

During the regularisation and rationalisation process, if the occupants were deemed to be in excess of the carrying capacity of the farm, some of the land occupants were moved to other farms that were either unoccupied or had space to accommodate more people. The physical occupation of the farms was therefore almost a guarantee that one would eventually be allocated land. As such, those who participated in the violent land occupations were more likely to be allocated land, and generally there

---

29 Interview with Mr FC, Provincial Administrator for Masvingo Province on 6 September 2010. There was no set time frame for the intervention by the government officials. On some of the farms, the intervention, regularisation and rationalisation was undertaken soon after the frenzy of the farm invasions and violence had subsided but on others (for example Masimbiti in Nuanetsi Ranch), the formal intervention had not been completed in April 2015 as I was winding up my field research.

were fewer women than men who participated in the violent farm invasions. Violence was an inhibiting factor for access to land by women.

Violence against women in resource conflict situations, including in relation to access, control and ownership of land is a global problem. The FAO notes that violence is often present in conflict and post-conflict situations, indeed the land itself is often a source of conflict (FAO, 2013:96). To address the challenge of violence against women in such issues, as in Zimbabwe, government and its institutions should create clear land policies, which recognise the rights of women to equality in accessing land. This should not apply to fast track land only, but to all land tenure systems, given that both structural and interpersonal violence have had an impact on women's land rights in the country.

In the communal areas, and Phase I resettlement areas for example, the continued failure by women to control land is defined more by structural violence than interpersonal violence as existing land governance structures continue to glorify the position of the man as the head of the household, and consequently the one who should be in control of the family land (Mushunje, 2001:Unpaginated). Women, on the other hand, continue to be expected to benefit from land through men, and as a result, they lose that benefit and access once the enabling relationship is no longer proximate. A combination of this structural violence and the interpersonal violence that accompanied the FTLRP has continued to disadvantage women in relation to access to land in the country. Unless such violence is acknowledged and addressed, women will continue to be the underdogs when it comes to land rights, access, ownership and control in the country.

5

Power and Law at Family, Local and National Levels

5.1 Introduction

In this chapter, I seek to address power within family structures and how this has impacted women's land rights under the FTLRP. I will examine the context of marriage, divorce and death, with a focus on women in different family and relational situations i.e. as daughters and wives during the various stages of a family cycle. The effect of divorce will focus on women as wives whilst the effect of death will consider women as both wives and daughters. Although other female relatives may also be affected in relation to access to land, the focus of this chapter will be on women who are closely related to a landholder or beneficiary of fast track land to the extent that they would be expected at law to directly benefit from the assets or estate of such a landholder during their lifetime and upon their death. As Von Benda Beckman et al., have noted:

> Property is the focus of struggles at all levels of social organization (levels of power), within and between families, communities, classes and States. The distribution of property objects has been contested throughout history and as have been the legal property regimes themselves (von Benda Beckman et al. 2006:2)

Thus it is clear that rights and entitlements over property are impermanent, fluid and can be impacted on by changes in life, social and community organisation, economic developments, marital standing and even legal imperatives. Changes occasioned by life events such as death and divorce can have considerable implications not only on human relationships but also on the relationships that people have with property. Such life changes can transform one's status and in the process their relationship with property that they previously had or had no connection with. The FAO emphasises that property should not be viewed as an object but as a relationship between (different) people and things (FAO, 2010:12). In this regard, the relationships between people play a significant role in determining their interaction and relationship with land.

Power relations also determine whether it is the law, or other normative frameworks that are used to determine rights, with different outcomes for differently situated people.

5.2 Post Fast Track Tenure Approaches

As the earlier chapters have shown, the chaotic manner in which the FTLRP was implemented meant that there was no defined tenure system in place at its inception. Neither did the courts have a clear framework to use in determining individuals' rights in relation to fast track land and, initially, they concluded that it was not part of the assets inventory upon divorce, as it was not part of matrimonial property but state land. Being generally reluctant to deal with an issue as contentious as fast track land, which could not be adjudicated upon by the courts, this argument provided a safe escape route. They often preferred to refer litigants to either the District Administrator's Office or the Ministry of Lands and Rural Resettlement for a determination of spouses' rights over fast track land. In other instances, other actors and institutions both formal and informal also made determinations on the rights of spouses to fast track land upon divorce. These included the war veterans, Committees of Seven, farm committees[1] and traditional leaders among others.

I interviewed officers representing the Zimbabwe Women Lawyers' Association (ZWLA) on the issue of women's rights to fast track land upon divorce and they expressed concern over the courts' refusal to adjudicate on fast track land for the reasons give above.[2] Challenges also

---

1 These were governance institutions that were created at individual farm level following the farm rationalisation and regularisation of farm occupations.
2 This still remains a challenge because the New 2013 Constitution maintains that courts have no jurisdiction over certain aspects of the fast track land such as compensation for acquired land (as opposed to improvements) and courts are not allowed to entertain any such cases (Section 72 (3) (b) of the Constitution).

arose because when people initially invaded and occupied commercial farmland, no discernible rights were given to the occupiers, other than government legislating for their protection from eviction by the white farmers.[3] The occupiers were subsequently given offer letters to acknowledge their occupation of the land, and some have since benefitted from more secure tenure through the issuance of permits for A1 farms and 99-year leases for A2 farms.

ZWLA officers were concerned that the courts were failing to create the much-needed jurisprudence on the issue of fast track land. Decisions by the courts would have been invaluable in setting out principles, rights and entitlements over the land early in the programme and thereby clarifying various unclear and contested issues. The premise is that the courts should be the last port of call in respect of any dispute and there should be no issue over which the courts have no jurisdiction. The ZWLA officials indicated that:

> There is therefore a gap in that in any dispute that cannot be resolved, the courts should be the last port of call and it is unnerving when the courts give the impression that there are certain cases that they cannot deal with.[4]

The reluctance by the courts to deal with fast track land and make determinations thereon can be explained because their jurisdiction was effectively undermined by constitutional amendment number 17 of 2005 (and maintained in the 2013 Constitution) which barred courts from hearing cases related to certain aspects of fast track land. In particular, they were barred from hearing cases challenging the compulsory acquisition of land or the amount of compensation to be paid except for improvements on the land.[5] These constitutional provisions were designed to ensure that the dispossessed white commercial farmers would not challenge the compulsory acquisition of their land or the attendant lack of compensation in the courts. However, the understanding and interpretation of this provision by the courts seemed to have extended to a general reluctance by the courts to make determinations on fast track land disputes, including in marriage settings. Their approach according

---

3   The 2001 Rural Land Occupiers (Protection from Eviction) Act [Chapter 20:26].
4   Interview with Abigail Matsvayi (ZWLA Programmes Co-ordinator) and Primrose Ratidzo Mungwari (ZWLA Legal Officer) on 6 November 2013.
5   Constitution of Zimbabwe, 2013, sec 72 (3) (b) and (c).

to ZWLA was similar to that used for immovable property in urban areas held in terms of an agreement of cession between an occupier and an urban local authority. The courts referred married couples to the local authorities to make determinations on occupation of the property in the event of a divorce instead of making a ruling themselves. Whilst the local authorities were able to decide on spouses' rights to urban-rented or rent-to-buy property in high density suburbs under the direct control of local urban housing authorities, in the case of fast track land, the default approach by the authorities was to recognise only the rights of the person in whose name an offer letter, permit or 99-year lease had been issued.

The result was that land rights of women were in some instances decided outside the judicial system. According to the Ministry of Lands and Rural Resettlement's Provincial Lands Officer in Masvingo,[6] their policy was that the person whose name appeared on the offer letter or lease would retain the piece of land in the event of a divorce. Where possible, the authorities would find alternative land for the excluded partner but this was not always possible; thus the losing partner often had to find an alternative place to live and an alternative means of livelihood. The practice of finding alternative land for the dispossessed should not be seen as a favourable outcome for the women concerned, as the Ministry of Lands and Rural Resettlement sought to suggest given the need to develop the new piece of land.

The ZWLA officers stressed that because men dominated the local farm level institutions, women often lost the fast track land to men in situations where determinations were made at that level. They stated that:

> There are clearly bilateral and multilateral social alliances of men to protect male privileges in the new resettlement areas. Men know each other socially and politically and they are well connected.[7]

According to ZWLA, the social capital and relationships that men enjoy on the farms are because they can freely interact in local spaces such as townships and beer halls as well as at political meetings (spaces of power) from which women are often excluded. Moreover, women's

---

6 Interview held on 12 February 2012 in Masvingo.
7 Interview with Abigail Matsvayi (ZWLA Programmes Coordinator) and Primrose Ratidzo Mungwari (ZWLA Legal Officer) on 6 November 2013.

gendered and domestic roles also limit their mobility and make it difficult for them to build relationships outside the home. Men, therefore, find it easier to support other men in the event of disputes over fast track land at the local level of power. That these same men dominated the institutions that made (and continue to make) determinations on access to fast track land in the event of divorce was also therefore detrimental to women.[8] I therefore conclude that the courts must be enabled to play their jurisprudential role in resolving land disputes if the rights of women are to be adequately protected.

5.3 Women's Rights to Fast Track Land in Marriage

This section looks at the role of marriage in securing or denying land rights for women. It evaluates the different types of marriage recognised by law in Zimbabwe and how women in different spousal contracts fared in accessing fast track land during marriage, upon divorce or upon death of the male landholder, be it a husband or father. A significant development since the conclusion of my research is the promulgation of the Zimbabwe Land Commission Act in February 2018 and its provision to the effect that fast track land shall be considered in line with the country's marriage and inheritance laws in the event of divorce or death.. Section 36 (5) of the Zimbabwe Land Commission Act states that:

> For the avoidance of doubt it is declared that the existing law on the devolution of property on marriage, dissolution of marriage, death ... shall apply to partially alienated State land except to the extent that different provision for such eventualities is expressly made by or under this Act or in a lease or permit issued under this Act or the repealed Agricultural Land Settlement Act.

Before passing this law in 2018, government had promulgated SI 53/2014 in terms of the Rural Land Act, which sought to apply similar principles in relation to A1 land. This is an unambiguous provision in relation to access and control over fast track land in all forms of allocation and in different family settings. Thus it represented a milestone for women's rights to fast track land, despite some noted flaws. This will be elaborated on further in the sections below.

---

8   Even though this was the case during my field research, the situation has largely remained the same.

5.3.1 Family level power relations in Monogamous Marriages

Women in monogamous marriages acquired land in their own right but also through their husbands with the majority of such women falling into the latter category. The acquisition of land through the husband meant that women had access to and could utilise the land but without any discernible control over it. The offer letter/permit or lease agreement for the piece of land was often in the name of the husband, with no strict requirements for land acquired by a married person to be registered in the name of both spouses during the early years of the programme.

At Chidza Farm, the respondents who had acquired land through their husbands were working on the land but relying on their husbands to make decisions about its utilization, such as what and when to plant; where and when to sell their produce and the quantities to be sold, etc. One of my respondents, a widow, Mrs RM2[9] indicated that she only had control over her land after the death of her husband. When he was still alive, he made all the decisions about the utilisation of the farm and the resultant produce. Although he 'consulted' her, the final decision always lay with him. Both she and her husband worked on the farm on a full-time basis. Another respondent,[10] also indicated that her husband made most of the decisions regarding land utilisation, the sale of produce (including livestock) and how the proceeds were to be allocated. She also said that although she was 'consulted', it was the husband's view that prevailed – a view shared by other women interviewed.[11]

The issue of men's 'power over' their wives at family level signified their control over the land, even land that was acquired by married women in their own right. When men assume control over land acquired by their wives by virtue of being the 'heads of households' it represents a clear case of invisible power. Similarly, women believed that even though they were the beneficiaries and recipients of land under the FTLRP, they could not make decisions regarding the control of this land when they had husbands. This state of affairs was explained away and justified on the basis of tradition, custom or social perception, beliefs which do not

---

9   She referred to herself as *Mbuya vaNomatter* (Nomatter's grandmother). Interview held on 9 September 2010 at Lothian Farm.
10 Interview held on 9 September 2010 at Lothian Farm.
11 For example, interviews with Mrs AM in Hippo Valley (Farm 54) on 6 February 2012, Mrs M7 in Nuanetsi Ranch (Masimbiti) on 11 March 2014 and Mrs AH in Hippo Valley (Mhlanganisi Farm) on 25 April 2011

allow women to be in control of property if they are married. In other instances, the economic wherewithal of the husband, especially when he was the one providing the farming inputs, meant that women allocated land in their own right could not control such land as they depended on their husbands to provide them with seed, fertiliser and draught power. In the application of the adage that 'he who pays the piper calls the tune', the wives deferred to their husbands as they provided the economic power driving production on the farms as their labour was regarded as comparatively valueless.

Mrs SG[12] reported during an interview that she was the one allocated land. At the time of the land invasions, her husband was working in Masvingo and could not leave his employment to camp on the farm. After the allocation, they made their new farm their main family home and she moved there with their nine children whilst her husband continued to work in town. He, however, provided the inputs that were required and visited the farm every weekend. During these visits, he would provide instructions on the activities to be undertaken during his absence i.e. when to start planting and harvesting, the variety of crops to be grown and the quantities of produce to be sold. The latter was sold under his name, mainly at the GMB in Masvingo, and the proceeds deposited into his bank account. As indicated above, he would 'consult' her on how the proceeds would be utilised but the final decision always lay with him. Following his death in 2009, she assumed total control of the farm.

Another dimension to the issue of control over the land and related activities by married women occurred when women were in charge either because of physical incapacity or lack of interest on the part of the husband. One of my respondents, Mrs C, was allocated a farm in the Hippo Valley Estates' Musisinyani area. She was the one who camped on the farm during the invasions as her husband was sick. A nurse by profession, Mrs C was also responsible for financing the farming activities and often visited the farm often to check on developments and give instructions to her farm manager and the other workers. She was in control of her land and everything that transpired on the farm because the husband's ill-health made it difficult for him to become involved. Another respondent, Mrs M1, was in control of her allocated land at Farm 54 in Hippo Valley Estates because her husband had no interest in farming. At the time of

---
12   Interview held with Mrs SG at Lothian Farm on 9 September 2010.

the interview,[13] he had died but she indicated that she had always been the one responsible for the farm because of her husband disinterest. As a result, she was the one to participate in the farm invasions and was subsequently allocated the piece of land. We can conclude that married women were either constrained or aided in controlling fast track land at the family level by:

  i. The framework governing the relationship between a husband and wife where the latter occupies a subordinate position and the former a dominant or controlling position;
  i. Societal attitudes (invisible power), which frowned upon women who controlled land and related processes when their husbands were alive and capable. The view is that as the 'head of the family', the husband must control land and its produce;
  i. Lack of resources, making women dependent on their husbands for inputs on the farms even in situations where the farm was acquired in the wife's name; and that
  i. Women had power and control over family land if the husband had no interest in the land or was incapacitated.

Despite these different forms of power with which women must engage in order to access and use land at the family level, SI 53/2014 is clear about landholding in a marriage for A1 allocations. Section 4 states that 'Every permit is issued for the benefit of the permit holder and his or her dependants'. As such both men and women in a marriage, as well as their children, are expected to benefit from such land, regardless of whether they are the permit holders or dependants of permit holders. The power dynamics however show that legal protections are inadequate on their own. They should be supported by education and awareness-raising to address issues of invisible power and capacitation so that women can engage with different forms and levels of power and in different spaces for the protection and enforcement of their rights.

5.3.2 Polygynous Marriages and Impact on Women's Land Rights

Despite a striking decline in the incidences of polygynous unions in Africa in the last half a century (Fenske, 2012:1), the practice is still commonplace though its form is often understood and practiced very differently. Traditionally, a polygynous man lived in the same compound

---
13 I held my first interview with Mrs M1 on 6 February 2012 in Chiredzi.

with his two or more wives. In modern day polygyny, the 'wives'[14] may live in different locations and even in different cities or countries as people adapt to contemporary realities. However, despite efforts to 'modernize' or adapt the practice of polygyny to modern day life, the CEDAW Committee views it as constraining women's rights and their dignity, and as a harmful cultural practice. Men however often justify polygamy as a good and acceptable cultural practice. The CEDAW Committee in General Recommendation Number 21 has noted that:

> Polygynous marriage contravenes a woman's right to equality with men, and can have such serious emotional and financial consequences for her and her dependents that such marriages ought to be discouraged and prohibited.[15]

The committee also raised concerns that despite many constitutions recognising the rights of women to be treated as equals with men, they also allowed polygyny on the basis of personal or customary law.[16] From their perspective, polygyny has negative implications for women's social, legal and economic wellbeing as the unequal power relations that exist in such 'marriages' weigh against their rights to property among other rights. The Committee regards the total abolition of polygyny as the best way of ensuring that women are not discriminated against, treated unequally or otherwise violated because of the continued recognition of polygyny as a form of marriage. The CEDAW approach differs from that taken by African States who while acknowledging that polygyny can have negative consequences regarding the rights of women, contend in the Maputo Protocol that:

> Monogamy is encouraged as the preferred form of marriage and that the rights of women in marriage and family, including in polygamous marital relationships are promoted and protected.[17]

In other words, they view the abolition of polygyny as a difficult task, which can only be achieved over time, if at all. Nyamu-Musembi agrees with this approach and argues that:

---

14 Rarely if ever is lobola paid or families known to each other. Indeed, often the relationships are quite clandestine, and commitments are rarely legalised.
15 Para 14.
16 Para 14.
17 Article 6 (c).

The CEDAW Committee can draw inspiration from the Maputo Protocol's approach in order to engage African States in a less stylized and more productive dialogue on legal pluralism: one that reflects an in-depth understanding of each country's context and each country's milestones along the path toward transformed gender relations (Nyamu-Musembi, 2013:213).

It is in the context of these different approaches that I consider the nature of the polygynous families that participated in the FTLRP. Six of my interviewees were in polygynous marriages, which in nearly all cases provided the trigger for their participation in the FTLRP. Five of the women told me that that they wanted to acquire property over which they could have control and leave for their children upon their death. The women feared that because of the polygynous nature of their marriages, the shrinking of the available farming land in the communal areas and the number of children that they were hoping would benefit from the same piece of land, there would be little or no land left for the children to build homes or farm. (The children also had limited chances of benefitting from any other available resources due to their numbers and the limited resources available.)

Although obtaining fast track land would not be the panacea to all their problems, it gave them an alternative to relying solely on their rural land. While having land that they could control was a factor for these women, it was notable that their main focus was not their own wellbeing but that of their children, in particular their sons.

For some women in polygynous relationships, access to a piece of land under the FTLRP was a means of escaping from a relationship where they felt excluded and in which their bargaining power over access to resources, including land for themselves and their children, was diminished. This applied to both first and subsequent wives, as they all understood that available land in the communal areas would need to be shared amongst all the sons. The FTLRP also provided opportunities to start lives outside often acrimonious polygynous unions.

Men in polygynous relationships sought land under the FTLRP for a variety of reasons. However, all such reasons were closely tied to the nature of their marriages. Polygyny was essentially a push factor in their decision-making and subsequent efforts to acquire land. Such issues or considerations included the following:

i. For men, it was sometimes the need to acquire more farming land for their wives in order to separate them as they were failing to live together harmoniously; and

ii. Some men saw polygyny as an accumulation strategy as the wives were able to establish themselves on separate farms while he maintained a hold on the original urban or communal home and overall, the family managed to acquire more land.

After the acquisition of the land, regardless of whether it was the men or the women in a polygynous marriage who had acquired it, the women if settled in different locations from their husbands, seemed to have more control over the land they were occupying. This was because the roving husband could not keep track of all the developments on the farms due to their prolonged absence. In a number of cases, a polygynous arrangement on the farms also differed significantly from the traditional polygynous set-up where the man stayed together with all his wives within the same homestead or compound and was therefore able to keep a tight leash on all the wives, monitor their movements and control their actions.

The traditional polygynous set-up also gave the man an opportunity to control his wives' labour and have more land under his control as each woman was given her own piece of land within the vicinity to cultivate with her children (Sen and Beneria, 1981:280, Peters and Peters, 1998:187). To an extent therefore, the desire by women in polygynous marriages to acquire land mirrored the traditional family land, economic and productive relations in Africa where women were required to work and provide for their individual households,[18] only contributing to the joint household of the man. As such, the efforts by women to assert their individual land needs under the FTLRP made sense and should provide a basis to argue for the individual allocation of land to women in polygynous relationships. Government policies against multiple farm ownership need to address what this means for polygynous marriages. Land allocation to a husband may not necessarily address the land needs of women in such relationships, even with joint registration.

Among my respondents, the friction that existed in polygynous marriages meant that wherever possible the wives tried to further their

---

18 Elizabeth A. Eldredge (1991), 'Women in Production: The Economic Role of Women in Nineteenth-Century Lesotho' *Signs*, Summer, 1991, Vol. 16, No. 4, Women, Family, State, and Economy in
Africa (Summer, 1991), pp. 707-731. University of Chicago Press.

interests and those of their children. Moreover that the women in these marriages played an active and often competitive role (against each other) over the acquisition of the land meant that the acquired land was registered in their own names to avoid the husband being identified as a multiple farm owner. To an extent this secured the women's access rights. As stated previously, the women were often driven by the need to ensure that on their death, the land could easily be claimed by their own children and not by the stepchildren, the husband or his other wife or wives. But effectively, more land was made available to the polygynous family.

5.3.3 Decision-making by women in polygynous marriages

Decision-making by married women is often inhibited as many decisions are deferred to the husband. This is particularly the case in African societies where the payment of the bride price implicitly means transferring power and decision-making from the woman to her husband and his family (Nii-Amoo Dodoo, 1998:233). In polygynous marriages, making decisions about critical issues is often a method used by men to maintain control over their two or more wives: independent decision-making often leads to greater independence for the women.

However, the fact that some women in polygynous marriages were able to settle in independent locations under the FTLRP and were not always under the direct control of their husbands made it easier for them to exercise significant independence and autonomy in decision-making. These ranged from deciding on the crops and hectarage to be planted and the utilisation of available resources including their time, a critical resource. Women could also make decisions about how to use the money after the sale of the farm produce. They would often seek ratification of their decisions by their husbands whom they normally consulted when making significant decisions such as building a house or purchasing farm equipment.

One of my respondents[19] showed significant autonomy and creativity on her sugar-cane plot. In addition to improving her rural home, she was able to use proceeds from her farming to acquire resources for the recapitalisation of the farm and for her own use. For example, although she could not drive, she bought a van to use on her farm and appointed her nephew as the driver. She also used the van to raise extra income

---

19 Name, initials and location with held at respondent's request.

by ferrying children to and from school. She charged USD10 per month per child and was contracted to provide this service for 41 children, thus earning $410/month. She was in complete control of the proceeds as she had bought the van and had the idea. She told me that she did not always disclose the full benefits of her business ventures to her husband, which provided her with extra income for other farming and self-improvement initiatives. The fact that her husband did not live nearby enabled her to make these autonomous but critical decisions that improved her farming and her standard of living.

As Grossbard has noted:

> Much of the recent literature in household economics has been critical of unitary models in which households act as monolithic blocs possibly led by a male benevolent dictator (Grossbard, 2011:42).

The criticism for this model is based on the realisation that households are often made up of individuals whose own preferences, constraints and choices are often to the detriment of other members of the household. Women and children are frequently the victims of such lineal decision-making processes that concentrates 'power over' in the so-called head of household. When women and other members of the household have the opportunity to make their own decisions, for their own benefit, the outcome is generally positive. Developments that encourage 'jointness' in decision-making or give women some level of autonomy are therefore preferable. The fact that women in polygynous relationships have managed to gain some leverage in decision-making under the FTLRP points to their emancipation, development and the economic and social wellbeing of their families.

5.4 Women's Rights to Fast Track Land upon Divorce

I have shown that the bulk of the land that was available under the FTLRP was acquired by and registered in the names of men, and that from the start and for many subsequent years, there was no clear policy to determine the rights of spouses over fast track land. This was due to lack of a clear tenure system or a guiding legal framework. Before the passage of the Zimbabwe Land Commission Act in 2016, it was difficult for the general laws applicable to matrimonial property and the rights of spouses upon divorce to be applied in respect of fast track land because such land was not considered as part of matrimonial property but state land.[20] The High Court in 2010 in *Chombo v Chombo* and in 2014 in *Chiwenga v Chiwenga*[21] cemented this position by ruling that spouses could not claim rights to fast track land registered in the other spouse's name upon divorce. The result was that upon divorce, the person in whose name the land was registered retained the land and the other spouse was required to leave without much debate.

S.I 53/2014 was promulgated in 2014. The Instrument was meant to address tenure rights and the rights of different categories of people in relation to fast track land in A1 allocations. The rights of spouses upon divorce were also addressed. In essence, S.I 53/2014 maintained the *status quo* in that the rights of the spouse in whose name the land is registered were maintained as superior. The only difference is that the exclusion of the non-registered spouse from fast track land has to be done following an elaborate procedure: previously the removal of such a spouse was automatic upon divorce. These provisions include 'buy-out'/compensation requirements and in some instances, arbitration and appeals procedures, which if fulfilled, allow the spouse in whose name the land is registered to retain it as of right.[22] This provision might appear fair in that it is gender neutral and will apply to either a male or female spouse. It is, however, discriminatory in effect given the gender skewed fast track land access patterns. The provision disproportionately and adversely affects women upon divorce in that they are the majority non-signatory permit holders under the programme and as such are prone to be evicted from fast track

---

20 Even whilst attempting to give rights to beneficiaries of fast track land, S.I 53/2014 emphasises that the land to which the permits relate remains state land as stipulated in Section 72 (4) of the Constitution of Zimbabwe, 2013.

21 Both men, Chombo and Chiwenga were two very senior political figures at the time and judges could well have been inhibited from making any other ruling. Indeed, the Supreme Court reached a different conclusion in relation to the Chombo case in 2018, after he lost his ministerial position following the 2017 coup. Chiwenga remains powerful, as the Vice President of the country and no contrary decision has been made by the courts regarding his case.

22 Section 14 (1) of S.I 53.2014 states that: 'If the marriage, or in the case of a polygynous marriage, any of the marriages between a permit holder who is the sole signatory of a permit and his or her spouse is dissolved, the non-signatory divorced spouse shall retain his or her rights as a joint permit holder or joint head of household unless the signatory permit holder compensates the divorced spouse for his or her assessed share under the permit'.

land upon divorce once the requisite compensation has been paid.

Conversely, due to a woman's lack of resources and their low economic status, women in whose names fast track land is registered can, in theory, be forced to remain with their divorced spouses after failing to meet the compensation requirements to buy out their spouses upon divorce. This is because the same Section 14 (1) clearly states that upon divorce, the non-signatory permit holder is entitled to retain his or her rights as a joint permit holder until compensation is paid. Thus, while the statutory instrument was a welcome development in that it clarified the basic tenurial issues and rights of spouses upon divorce, the *de facto* discrimination suffered by women upon divorce in terms of access to and benefit from fast track land continued. As such by giving women rights, similar to those enjoyed by men without addressing the structural inequalities and disadvantages that women face *per se*, the statutory instrument failed to move women forward in terms of access to land in Zimbabwe. As Fredman has noted:

> It is not sufficient simply to extend socio-economic rights to women. Instead, socio-economic rights need to be recast in light of the demands of substantive gender equality. Substantive gender equality goes beyond treating women in the same way as men and requires transformative measures (Fredman, 2009:410-411).

In line with the above, a point to make is that despite the reality that S.I 53/2014 offered an opportunity for government to correct the gender skewed land access patterns under the FTLRP by compelling joint registration and joint signing of fast track land permits by spouses, joint registration still remains optional under this law. While a qualifying spouse or spouses are considered as joint permit holders or joint heads of household, it is not a requirement that they be jointly registered as signatory permit holders. The discrimination in these provisions arises in the event of divorce, where the signatory permit holder is accorded stronger rights than the non-signatory permit holder/joint head of household.

The relevant A1 permit registration form as provided for in S.I 53/2014 is provided overleaf:

Agricultural Land Settlement (Permit Terms and Conditions) Regulations, 2014

This Permit is issued subject to the terms and conditions set out in the Agricultural Land Settlement (Permit Terms and Conditions) Regulations, 2014.

DETAILS OF PERMIT HOLDER

For the purposes of this section, a "Permit Holder" means a male or female head of household in whose name this Permit is issued. The Permit Holder in whose name this Permit is issued shall be primarily responsible for fulfilling the conditions of this Permit.

However, despite the fact that the Permit is issued to the person named in this section, the spouse of the Permit Holder or, in the case of a polygamous marriage, all the spouses of the Permit Holder (as specified under section 2.1), shall be regarded as Joint Heads of Household for the purposes of this Permit.

1.1 Surname: ....
1.2 First name: ....
1.3 Other names: ....

1.4 Title (Dr./Mr./Mrs./Miss/Ms.): ....
1.5 Place of birth:
....

1.6 Date of birth: .... Age: ....
1.7 National ID Number: ....

| 1.8 | Marital Status (*tick applicable*): .... | Married | Single | Divorced | Widowed |

1.9 Citizenship: ....

IN THE CASE OF JOINT SIGNATORIES:

1.1 Surname: ....
1.2 First name: ....
1.3 Other names: ....

1.4 Title (Dr./Mr./Mrs./Miss/Ms.): ....
1.5 Place of birth: ....
1.6 Date of birth: .... Age: ....
1.7 National ID Number: ....

Source: Statutory Instrument 53/2014

The fact that spouses are regarded as joint permit holders and joint heads of household (as opposed to joint signatory permit holders) does not give them equal rights to the land upon divorce but still gives the signatory permit holder superior rights. With the passing of the Zimbabwe Land Commission Act, however, the legal position is that sharing of fast track land upon divorce in the absence of contrary provisions in the Act or a lease or permit must be determined by the courts in line with the provisions of Sec 7 (4) of the Matrimonial Causes Act: Chapter 5:13. This was the position taken by the Supreme Court in the *Chombo v Chombo*[23] case on appeal from the High Court. Two issues were under consideration, by the Supreme Court, namely:

i. Whether in terms of the Matrimonial Causes Act, the parties' rights in the leased farm could be distributed on divorce; and

ii. If they could be distributed what would be a fair and equitable distribution of those rights.

In allowing the appeal and remitting the case to the *court a quo* (High Court) to distribute the parties' interests and rights in the 99-year lease, the Supreme Court came to the following conclusions:

i. Even though the court could not distribute or share the farm, which was the preserve of the Executive as the farm belonged to government, the spouses' rights in the 99-year lease were an asset of the spouses, which needed to be distributed in terms of sec 7 (4) of the Matrimonial Causes Act; and

ii. The Supreme Court urged the *court a quo* to take into account all the provisions of the Matrimonial Causes Act in distributing the rights and interests of the parties in the 99-year lease, including the fact that the wife had contributed both directly and indirectly in the acquisition of the 99-year lease, given that it was awarded during the subsistence of the marriage.

This decision finally clarified the critical issue of spousal rights to fast track land upon divorce. Although the decision came eighteen years late, when women had suffered considerably due to lack of clarity and jurisprudence on the issue, it is a positive development that should provide certainty and protection to women's rights to fast track land upon divorce. S.I 53/2014 therefore requires revisiting to ensure that it

---

23 SC 41/18, Civil Appeal No. SC 326/14) [2018] ZWSC 41.

complies with the pronouncements of the Supreme Court in this case, and the provisions of Sec 36 (5) of the ZLC Act. In particular, it needs to ensure that spousal rights in fast track land are determined in terms of the Matrimonial Causes Act, and that no spouse gets automatic rights over matrimonial property, such as rights in land at divorce.

When sharing property or granting an order of maintenance upon granting a decree of divorce, Sec 7 of Matrimonial Causes Act requires the courts to consider the following:

i. The income-earning capacity, assets and other financial resources which each spouse and child has or is likely to have in the foreseeable future;
ii. The financial needs, obligations and responsibilities which each spouse and child has or is likely to have in the foreseeable future;
iii. The standard of living of the family, including the manner in which any child was being educated or trained or expected to be educated or trained;
iv. The age and physical and mental condition of each spouse and child;
v. The direct or indirect contribution made by each spouse to the family, including contributions made by looking after the home and caring for the family and any other domestic duties;
vi. The value to either of the spouses or to any child of any benefit, including a pension or gratuity, which such spouse or child will lose as a result of the dissolution of the marriage; and
vii. The duration of the marriage.

Additionally, in sharing property or granting an order of maintenance upon divorce, the 'court shall endeavour as far as is reasonable and practicable and, having regard to their conduct, is just to do so, to place the spouses and children in the position they would have been in had a normal marriage relationship continued between the spouses'. Effectively, therefore, the court when dealing with fast track land upon divorce is guided by what is fair and just, looking at the circumstances of each case. The mere fact that land is registered in the name of one party to a marriage is no longer an automatic guarantee for the enjoyment of superior rights over that land by the registered party. Coupled with the current position taken by the Ministry of Lands, Agriculture, Water and Rural Resettlement to register fast track land acquired by a married person in the names of both (or all spouses in the case of a polygynous marriage), it is clear that the position of women in relation to access to land in the country is improving. It also follows that the provisions of S.I 53/2014 giving superior land rights to the signatory permit holder are *ultra vires* the enabling Act (The Zimbabwe Land Commission Act repealed the Rural Land Act under which the SI was made) and must therefore be rendered invalid.

However, these rights must be extended to communal land as well, if the women's land rights are to be further protected. The FAO (1994) reports that despite the progress that Zimbabwe has made in terms of women's rights, including being a State Party to CEDAW, challenges still remain in certain aspects of women's land and property rights amongst other rights. The organisation notes that:

> However, women still do not have equal access to land in the communal areas. Married women have only secondary land use rights through their husbands, and divorced women are required to vacate the land and acquire new land in their natal homes.[24]

This position was entrenched by the courts in Zimbabwe through decided court cases. In the case of *Khoza v Khoza* (HC-B-106-87), the wife upon divorce was deprived of the couple's communal land home despite the fact that she was solely responsible for the development and upkeep of the home while her husband was working in the city. In denying the wife access to the rural matrimonial home and giving her the city house despite the fact that farming was her only means of livelihood, the court argued that the patrilocal nature of rural Zimbabwean life made it difficult for the wife to remain amongst her husband's relatives after their divorce. As Gopal and Salim note:

> This case demonstrates the risks arising from the derivative nature of women's access to communal land. The woman could not retain her rural home and the right to reside there and cultivate the fields because her right was perceived as derivative and contingent upon her status as a wife, and therefore terminated upon divorce (Gopal and Salim, 1998:95).

---

24 http://www.fao.org/docrep/v9101e/v9101e04.htm

Therefore, this illustrates the need for the provisions of the Matrimonial Causes Act to be extended to all property of the parties, regardless of the nature of the property or whether it is held in terms of customary or general law. In addition, the fact that the provisions of the Matrimonial Causes Act do not apply to unregistered customary law unions, leave a significant number of women exposed and unprotected. This is particularly concerning given that estimates show that the bulk of 'marriages' in the country are unregistered. In 2013, the country's Deputy Registrar General, Ms Locadia Majonga was quoted as saying that 84% of 'marriages' in Zimbabwe are unregistered.[25] Her remarks reveal the staggering number of women that are exposed by the stratification of marriages with some given superior rights over others.

The current efforts to have just one law on marriages is a welcome development. A composite Marriage Bill is currently before Parliament.[26] It seeks to have one marriage law and to give equal protection to all marriages, including unregistered customary law unions. To its credit and despite some of its flaws, S.I 53/2014 has already recognised unregistered customary law unions. In its definition section, it provides that '[spouse]' includes 'a spouse in an unregistered customary law marriage, and 'marry' shall be construed accordingly' thereby giving acknowledgement to a marriage regime, which despite being the most prevalent, has not previously been given appropriate recognition.

5.5 Women's Right to Fast Track Land Upon Death of a Husband

There is a general, even though sometimes reluctant, acceptance by the population in Zimbabwe that upon the death of a spouse, the surviving spouse should inherit the deceased's property, including land.[27] Respondents interviewed on the issue including village heads,[28] government officials,[29] senior community opinion leaders,[30] as well as the fast track land beneficiaries, both men and women, accepted this

---

25 *The Herald*, '84pc of Zim marriages unregistered' (Harare, 6 February 2013).
26 By May 2020, the Bill had reached the Committee Stage.
27 Traditionally the deceased husband's family would inherit the property and the widow too was required to be 'inherited' by the deceased husband's brothers or other relatives in order to access the property or to be looked after.
28 Village Head M2, interviewed at Chidza Farm on 10 March 2014.
29 Mr DM, Provincial Lands Officer interviewed in Masvingo on 10 February 2012.
30 Mr CM, interviewed in Masimbiti, Nuanetsi Ranch on 14 March 2014.

principle as law and practice, especially if the women had children with their deceased husbands. The reason for supporting the woman to continue utilising the land in such a situation was that she was using the land to raise the children and also that she was holding the land as a caretaker in order for the children to take over when they were older.

A school headmaster whom I interviewed in the Masimbiti area argued that whilst he was against the idea of his wife taking over the land in the event of a divorce, he had no problem with her keeping the land upon his death because she would use the land to raise their children. He was clearly against the idea of his siblings or other relatives taking the land from his wife after his death.

Many of my respondents were widows who had remained on the farms following the death of their husbands. Despite the cultural constraints that they faced in relation to the land following the death of the husbands, they were still able to keep the land. One of my respondents' challenges was that she could not change the land registration documents into her name without the 'blessings' of the deceased husband's family. She had to travel to the rural home to request permission to change the registration documents in person because she believed that this was a significant issue that required her to show respect to her in-laws by discussing it in person. However, because she did not manage to make the journey to the village for a long time, the farm remained registered in her deceased husband's name, even though no one had stopped her from changing the registration documents. At the time of concluding my field research, she still had undisturbed possession of the farm and was able to continue with her farming activities. Her failure to change the landholder details for the farm into her name were informed more by the invisible power wrought by customary and cultural beliefs, which made it difficult for her to accept that she could do so without authority of her deceased husband's family.

Both the Zimbabwe Land Commission Act and S.I 53/2014 recognise the rights of widows/widowers to fast track land. The import of Sec 36 (5) of the Act is that upon death of a landholder, fast track land will devolve according to the country's inheritance laws such as the Administration of Estates Act, [Chapter 6:01] and the Deceased Estates Succession Act, [Chapter 6:02]. The Administration of Estates Act recognises unregistered customary law unions for purposes of inheritance. It states that:

> A marriage contracted according to customary law shall be regarded as a valid marriage for the purposes of this Part notwithstanding that it has not been solemnized in terms of the Customary Marriages Act [Chapter 5:07], and any reference in this Part to a spouse shall be construed accordingly.[31]

This, of course, shows the dichotomy that still exists in the country with regard to differentiated recognition of the unregistered customary law union at divorce and at death, as elaborated above in relation to the application of sec 7 (4) of the Matrimonial Causes Act. In essence, it shows reluctance by law makers to allow men and women to share property on the basis of equality at divorce, although there is a level of acceptance for women to inherit the property upon the death of the husband.

S.I 53/2014 states that upon the death of a signatory permit holder, his or her rights under the permit shall:

> In the case of a monogamous or potentially polygamous marriage where there is an existing or surviving spouse, devolve to the existing or surviving spouse.[32]

In the case of a polygamous marriage, the wives are also entitled to inherit those rights in equal and undivided shares.[33]

As noted above, the S.I recognises unregistered customary law unions. Together with the provisions of the Administration of Estates Act, which also recognises such unions, women/wives now have stronger legal protections and rights to inherit fast track land.

The application of these positive provisions is however tempered by the ruling in the *Chigwada* case, as discussed below, regarding the rights of a spouse to give away his or her property in a will to the exclusion of the surviving spouse. Given this development, I suggest that the courts should not simply consider the issue of registration of property as a determinant of ownership of or rights in property, but also appraise the actual contribution made towards the acquisition of the property made by a surviving spouse. The same questions, asked at divorce in terms of contribution towards the acquisition of property to ascertain the parties' shares, should also be asked on the dissolution of a marriage by death, in

---

31 Sec 68 (3).
32 Sec 13 (1) (a).
33 Sec 13 (1) (c).

order to determine each spouse's property and ultimately the deceased estate. When a spouse writes a will, there is need to determine what he or she can give away as his or her sole property from the matrimonial assets. The question therefore is 'what constitutes a deceased estate' in situations where the testator was married? Is it everything that was registered in his or her name, or only that which he or she acquired, or contributed in acquiring through both direct and indirect means?

Sec 5 (3) (a) of the Wills Act states that:

> No provision, disposition or direction made by a testator in his will shall operate so as to vary or prejudice the rights of – any person to whom the deceased was married to a share in the deceased's estate or in the spouses' joint estate in terms of any law governing the property rights of married persons.

Read together with sec 2 of the Married Persons Property Act, which provides for an out of community of property marriage regime in Zimbabwe, the argument can be advanced to limit what a married person can dispose of in a will. Even if the property in question is registered in the name of the testator, the contribution of the other spouse (or spouses in a polygamous marriage) must be considered before a determination is made on whether a testator has only bequeathed his or her sole property.

A second or alternative approach is for Zimbabwe to have a law that limits freedom of testation to provide the matrimonial home and household goods and effects with the same protections they are given in intestate succession. This provision should have a basic stipulation to the effect that regardless of the type of marriage, a married testator cannot bequeath the matrimonial home and household goods and effects to any person other than their spouse. In respect of fast track land, this would entail that if the land in question is also the matrimonial home, then such land cannot be given away in a will to any person other than the spouse (or spouses) of the testator as appropriate and subject to reasonable exceptions.

5.6 Women as Daughters

Traditionally, the economic and social value of children in Zimbabwe as in many other societies has been determined by their gender. Male children have been/are considered more valuable because they would stay within and look after their natal homes, presumably look after their parents in old age and bear children to keep the family name alive. On the other hand, female children are expected to get married, with the parents collecting bride-wealth and then consigning the young women to their husbands' families. The low value attributed to female children in Zimbabwean society during the colonial period was reflected in the parents' reluctance to spend resources on educating female children due to the perception that they would use their education to develop their husbands' families. The view as Schmidt notes was that:

> A son could work, providing his parents with a range of material advantages, but a daughter could only marry. All her subsequent labour would be for her husband and his kin. In the case of girls, parents reasoned, there was no return in investment (Schmidt, 1991:141).

This view of a female child as a transient member of her natal family still exists in Zimbabwean society today and has the effect of denying women access to resources as daughters. This is despite the fact that research has shown that female children are more inclined to look after their parents in their old age , both in terms of physical caring and provision of economic resources, than their male counterparts (Matikiti et al., 2018:33). Research by the American Sociological Association (ASA) concluded that: 'Daughters provide as much elderly parent care as they can [whilst] sons do as little as possible' (ASA, 2014:1).

The notion that daughters are a wasted investment does not seem to bear scrutiny. Despite this reality, however, my research revealed some of the challenges that daughters face in accessing land acquired under the FTLRP by both their mothers and fathers. With the phrase *'ivhu ndiyo nhaka'* translated to mean *'land is the real inheritance'* being used by both male and female beneficiaries of the FTLRP, with few exceptions, it was clear that the beneficiaries would prefer to hand down land to their sons not their daughters. This attitude was shared regardless of level of education, economic or social status. The position of married daughters was almost certain. They could not inherit or be given land under any circumstances because that would amount to giving family land to the son-in-law and his family. A Village Head in Chidza Farm, a father of five boys and three girls had this to say:

> I would give a son a piece of land and not a girl because the son *ndiye mwene womusha* (he is the rightful owner of the home). I would only give land to a daughter if she was divorced or widowed and decides to come back to stay with me simply because I cannot chase her away. If my daughter decides to come back with her husband on this farm, I would not entertain them, because I cannot look after a son-in-law. He has his own family and they will think that I am alienating their son from them. In our culture, a son-in-law cannot stay in the natal home of his wife.[34]

Chidza Farm's previous owner, Mr Bollard, was rearing Brahman cattle on the farm at the time of the farm invasions and the subsequent allocation of land and he was allowed by the government to keep 500 hectares of the farm. He therefore lived side by side with the new settlers until the time of his death when his daughter had taken over the farm and was running it with her husband. I asked the Village Head why he found it difficult to leave his farm to his daughters when Mr Bollard had left his farm to his daughter. His answer was simple, Mr Bollard had no sons and therefore had no choice but to leave the farm to a daughter. If he had had sons, he too would have left the farm to them. His view was that the decision to leave valuable property to sons ran across cultures and was not only a black Zimbabwean or African issue. In other words, patriarchy knows no race or national boundaries. In describing sexism in South Africa, the former Constitutional Court Judge, Justice Albie Sachs, had this to say:

> It is a sad fact that one of the few profoundly non-racial institutions in South Africa is patriarchy. Amongst the multiple chauvinisms, which abound in our country, the male version rears itself with special and equal vigour in all communities. Indeed, it is so firmly rooted that it is frequently given a cultural halo and identified with the customs and personality of different communities. Thus, to challenge patriarchy, to dispute the idea that men should be the dominant figures in the family and society, is seen not to be fighting against male privilege but as attempting to destroy African tradition or subvert Afrikaner ideals or undermine civilized and decent British values (Sachs, 1990:1).

The unfortunate reality is that the perpetuation of patriarchy and the

---
34 Interview with Village Head M 2 in Chidza Farm on 10 March 2014.

acceptance of the superiority of men over women is not an issue only perpetrated by men, but women have also internalised this viewpoint, a clear example of invisible power at play. In consequence, female respondents during my field research were of the view that female children should not inherit fast track land but that it should be given to their male siblings. It was only after being challenged about the effect of this approach, given their own role as women in the land acquisition process, that they would reluctantly concede that female children should receive similar treatment to that given to their brothers.

The inheritance laws cited above, coupled with the Constitution's equality and non-discrimination provision,[35] provide daughters with equal opportunities to inherit land from their parents and utilise it during their parents' lifetime as equals with their brothers. Stereotypical attitudes, however, remain, and these need to be challenged to ensure that the rights of women as daughters are not overlooked in relation to any land in the country, including fast track.

5.7 Conclusion

The improvement in the legal, policy and constitutional framework for women's rights to access land generally, and under the FTLRP specifically, has the potential to improve their and their families' wellbeing, and tangentially that of women generally. Women in the agricultural sector are workers of the land and their productivity would surely increase if they were to have control over that land and be in a position to make decisions about its utilisation. Currently, the bulk of the land under the FTLRP is in the hands of men, though women can still benefit through inheritance from fathers, husbands and other male relatives or as part of a settlement upon divorce or separation. My research, however, reveals that there is still reluctance by both parents to give property to female children or other female relatives, whether as inheritance or donations. The insistence on male children as heirs and recipients of fast track land does not however necessarily translate into uptake or utilisation of the land by the male children, as some of them may not be interested in farming. The result is that foisting such land on the sons, leads to underutilisation or non-utilisation of the land.

Another observation was that married women are better off following

---

35 Sec 56 (3).

the death of a husband (in intestate succession as the law stands) than at divorce or separation with regards to access to fast track land. This is because there is general societal acceptance that wives must inherit their husbands' property upon death, but this view is not shared with regard to divorce or separation. The existence of fairly strong laws on women's intestate inheritance rights and the popularisation of the laws by both the government and NGOs has gone a long way towards furthering this attitude, as have the generally high levels of education in the country, with inheritance law and rights being taught even at primary school level.[36]

The same robust approach has not been adopted with regards to women's property rights upon divorce. The result is that programmes such as the FTLRP have attempted to come up with clearer and favourable policies or practices with regards to women's inheritance to fast track land, but often lack similar clarity or favourable provisions with regards to women's rights to the same land upon divorce or separation. The fact that joint spousal registration on 99-year leases is governed by the Ministry of Lands' Policy and not necessarily a specific legal provision is testimony to this anomaly. The initial reluctance by the courts to protect women's rights to fast track land upon divorce was similarly anomalous.

The resistance inherent at national, legal, institutional and societal level for the wholesale acceptance of the need to treat women as equals with men is displayed in the selective approach by various actors and structures with regards to which rights to grant to women and which ones to withhold. Where women's rights step on the toes of male privilege, in particular, such as with divorce or separation, they are frowned upon, but if no manly rights are affected, for example, when the husband has died, then the women often can enjoy the manly privileges and benefits, including accessing the man's economic resources. The Zimbabwe Land Commission Act, whilst providing that marriage laws must apply to the devolution of fast track land upon death or divorce, fails to recognise co-registration of the same land as an important aspect in protecting the spouses' rights to that land. Effectively, the outcome is that at both law and in practice, women are better able to access land held by their husbands upon the husbands' death in intestate succession compared to a situation of divorce or separation.

---

36 Interview with Mr CM, a Headmaster in Nuanetsi Ranch in March 2014.

In testate succession, the law has been further complicated by the recent case of *Chigwada v Chigwada*[37] (delivered on 28 December 2020). In this case, a husband bequeathed his half share in the matrimonial home, which was jointly registered with his wife, to a son from a previous marriage. The Supreme Court confirmed that the *de facto* marriage regime in Zimbabwe is out of community of property and as such each partner in such a relationship builds and grows his or her own estate during the subsistence of a marriage. Consequently, a spouse is at liberty to disinherit his or her spouse as long as the spouse making the will is only disposing of his share of the property in the matrimonial estate. The court concluded that:

> To deny a person married out of community of property the right to dispose of his or her property by will to whomsoever he or she chooses is to erode the foundation on which the doctrine of freedom of testation lies.[38]

Following this reasoning and sec 36 (5) of the Zimbabwe Land Commission Act,[39] permits and leases that are issued by government for fast track land should expressly state that a surviving spouse shall inherit such land despite the existence of a will which may make contrary provisions. The current provisions in both SI 53/2014 and sec 36 (5) of the ZLC Act seem to apply only in intestate inheritance.

Girl children, though catered for under principles of non-discrimination in the Constitution of Zimbabwe of 2013 and in the provisions of S.I 53/2014 are in reality still disadvantaged. The general perception is that daughters, especially married ones, cannot inherit agricultural land. The approach with regards to other forms of property, including immovable property in urban areas, is more flexible. The cultural value that is placed on agricultural land *'ivhu'* means that both mothers and fathers generally prefer that such land be given to male children as they are seen as being in a position to keep the land within the family.

6

Women, Power and Decision-Making for Access to and Control over Land

6.1 Introduction

This chapter seeks to analyse the power and decision-making processes that different women engaged with at various stages of the FTLRP. The underlying assumption is that the dominant power relations and decision-making processes that were at play at various levels during the FTLRP undermined women's opportunities and capacities to effectively participate in and benefit from the FTLRP. This supposition is held in the understanding that different women had different capacities and were differently situated, resulting in differentiated outcomes.. As such, in many instances there was no *de jure* discrimination between women and women and between men and women in terms of the normative rules, but the fact that they were differently situated in the world in which the rules operated is what resulted in discrimination for many women in reality (Farha, 2008:561). Ikdahl aptly captures the dynamics of unequal power relations between men and women by stating that legislation addressing the issue of land and property is often gender neutral, but in reality it interacts with gendered local norms (Ikdahl, 2013:169). This resonates with the position taken by Dahl, (1987:51) that Women's Law must be cognisant of the relationship between 'law in books' and 'law in action'. This means that male cultural hegemony has to be overcome, more particularly because it is often accepted as normal, even by those that are subordinated by it (Dahl, 1987:3).

Thus, there is need to understand the inequality and discrimination fundamentals that are usually at play in land reform, redistribution and access processes to ensure that women's rights and needs are not overlooked and lost during these processes. Levels of access to resources, nature of property rights and the quality of property that is accessible to men and women are indicators in understanding the implications of gender inequality and discrimination as well as unbalanced power relations on women's property rights. As Hirschon points out:

> Much feminist writing is in essence an attempt to grapple with issues of power in the relative positions of women and men. Whether expressed in terms of patriarchy, sexual asymmetry, female subordination or male dominance, questions regarding power lie at the heart of many discussions of gender relations. The issues related to power involve the ability to act autonomously, to command compliance from others or to control their actions. In this respect 'property', however it is approached and whatever its constituents, is a crucial indicator of the balance of power between women and men (Hirschon, 1984:1).

The above observation by Hirschon needs to be juxtaposed with the position of women in Zimbabwe, in particular, under the FTLRP, when analysing issues of autonomy, command and compliance that women had to wrestle with in respect of their relationships with men as individuals and men as groups in families, communities and decision-making structures that existed in male-dominated national and local land-related institutions. Power relations and decision-making processes are critical facets of any social, political and economic transformative process as was the FTLRP. This is because such a process of transformation must accomplish the 'eradication of gender biases in access to and control over economic resources, and in the decision-making processes that shape policies' (Opendemocracy.net, 4), including those relating to land and the economy. Power, whether ideological, political, economic or social has the effect of giving some people greater authority over definitions and interpretations compared to others (Agarwal, 1997:21). In the case of women and access to resources, such definitions and interpretations can have the effect of sidelining them from the processes that enable access to resources.

The power and decision-making analysis in this chapter will consider all the different levels, from local to international. It is recognised that international power dynamics and relationships in particular between Zimbabwe as a nation state and the international community had a crucial bearing on the manner in which the FTLRP was implemented. This, in turn, had implications for women at the local level. It is therefore necessary to engage with and understand the decision-making and power relations at the various levels and during the different stages of the land reform programme because high-level decision-making processes and actors during the FTLRP had implications on the decisions that were taken by women at a very local level. In making this analysis, one has to be conscious that rights' claiming can be a highly political process as opposed to a legalistic or technical one (Andreassen and Crawford, 2013: 5). It should also be understood that decisions that are taken at a very high level, especially those that are politically inclined can be reached without regard to the technical or legal imperatives that must normally guide decision-making. However, although such decisions are taken at the highest level, they normally affect citizens on the lowest rungs of the social, political and economic strata. Women are often negatively affected by such decisions because of their concentration at the lowest of these rungs. In this chapter, I will also seek to assess international high-level decision-making processes and how women, whether as individuals or groups, engaged with power at the international level. Such engagement with high-level power will be analysed for its implications on women on the farms and in the villages as they sought to engage with the land reform programme and the attendant power dynamics at the local and family levels.

6.2 Formal Equality, Discriminatory Reality

The FTLRP at the political level gave the impression that every black Zimbabwean who was in need of land was eligible to access land as long as they wanted the land (Machingura, 2012:267). Theoretically, therefore, both men and women were supposed to benefit equally from the land reform programme but in reality women were side-lined (Stewart and Damiso, 2013:468). With slogans such as *'ivhu kuvanhu'* (land to the people), dominating the discourse at the political level, the impression at face value was that this was a programme for everyone and that land would be easy to obtain. By 2005, the Constitution of Zimbabwe had been amended to provide that women must be treated on the basis of equality with men in relation to access to resettlement land. Ostensibly, therefore, at this stage in the land reform process, there was no discrimination in accessing land as long as one was an indigenous Zimbabwean. In reality, however, both gender and racial discrimination existed and still exist in Zimbabwe's approach to access to agricultural land, sometimes covertly and sometimes more overtly. In terms of gender-related access to land, the gender-neutral assertions have been and continue to be met with gendered realities and power relations that make it difficult for women to compete for land as equals with men. In fact, in contemporary societies, such a seemingly inclusive approach is what allows discrimination to fester. This is because it is hidden behind the non-discriminatory language of laws, policies and practice (Farha, 2008:561). The effect is gender-neutral laws that result in de facto discrimination as the law fails to correspond to women's lived reality and needs (Dahl, 1987:12).

As Andreassen and Crawford note:

> Rights are often denied in the first place by structural inequalities and dominant power relations, and that realising rights is thus dependent on addressing and challenging those same structural inequalities and power relations in ways that shift the distribution of power in society in favour of relatively poor and marginalised groups (Andreassen and Crawford, 2013: 5).

In the case of the FTLRP, this state of affairs must also be viewed with the understanding that the claims for land by women were made in a plural legal environment with various norms, laws, actors and structures displaying often-overlapping power and decision-making authority. The plural nature of the interactions had both positive and negative outcomes for women, even though the negatives outweighed the positives as will be detailed below.

6.3 Women's Organisations Engaging with Visible Power at the National and International Levels and Hidden Power at the Local Level

Earlier chapters provided a background to the land question in Zimbabwe from the colonial period through to the implementation of the FTLRP with a particular focus on the legal, policy, social and economic imperatives that have informed access to land in the country over the years. Here, the focus is narrowed to the policy and decision-making processes around the FTLRP and how women engaged with them. These processes were influenced by the state's position at the national level and its obligations and interactions at the international level as influenced by international human rights law and rule of law considerations. However, decisions made at this level regarding the country's FTLRP had implications for women especially in relation to their interaction with the process and their rights and ability to equally acquire land. At the same time the complexities of engagement at this level made it difficult for individual women to engage with visible state power and the international community, leaving such tasks to women's groups and women's rights organisations such as the Women and Land Lobby Group (WLLG) and the Zimbabwe Women Lawyers Association (ZWLA) among others. These organisations were perceived as having the skills and resources to engage with and influence visible power for the benefit of the generality of women in the country. However, whilst efforts were made to engage with visible power, the highly contested, chaotic and often violent manner in which the FTLRP was implemented created a murky policy, legal and implementation environment. This made it hard to easily identify the sources and holders of power and decision-makers at the local level.

With the understanding that gender neutral laws on their own were not adequate in providing a level playing field for access to land by women, the women's rights organisations made efforts to engage with visible state power in an effort to ensure substantively equal treatment for women. The engagement started at the point of conceptualisation of Phase II of the Land Reform and Resettlement Implementation Plan through to the FTLRP. The WLLG, ZWLA and the ZWRCN were some of the organisations that engaged with visible state power to address women's needs. Whilst ZWLA, (established in 1992) and the ZWRCN (established in 1990) had long been in existence at the time of implementation of the FTLRP, the WLLG was formed in 1998 by women, with support from donors, with the sole objective of ensuring women's rights to access land under the country's land reform and redistribution programme. ZWLA and ZWRCN, on the other hand, were specialist general women's rights, gender and development organisations and as such were mandated by their objectives to address any such issues.

The establishment of the WLLG occurred at the height of policy formulation and discussions towards the implementation of Phase II of the Land Reform and Resettlement Programme. Some of the strategies used by the Group to capture the attention of the state and its institutions included critical analysis of state policies on land reform, analysis of relevant laws and the Constitution and their implications on the equal treatment of women. They also organised public meetings to which they invited state officials to address women about their land rights and provide feedback to state institutions. For example, the WLLG was one of only five national civil society, agricultural and business organisations to address the all-important 1998 International Donors' Conference on Land Reform and Resettlement, thereby showing its capacity to engage with visible power at the highest level. Subsequently, on 9 August 2000, the WLLG organised a meeting for women at the Sheraton Hotel in Harare, and invited the then Vice President of Zimbabwe, Joseph Msika, to address women on their land rights (Hellum and Derman, 2000:15).

ZWRCN started working on the issue of women's rights to land in 1994 with their active participation in the Mandivamba Rukuni led Land Commission from 1994-98 and in the subsequent government's Justice Chidyausiku led Constitutional Review Commission which resulted in the rejected 2000 draft constitution (Essof and Chigudu, 2004). ZWLA with its specialist legal footprint led the legal reform agenda on the rights of women with a focus on Section 23 of the 1980 Independence Constitution, which permitted discrimination on the basis of personal or customary law, a provision that could be used to deny women access to land under the FTLRP. The ZWLA advocacy process for the amendment of Section 23 began in 1999 with the Chidyausiku Commission wherein individual ZWLA members lobbied for the amendment of the Section (Hellum, 2013:35). Goebel (2006:143) notes that this engagement led to concessions in the development of land reform policy documents that recognised the rights of women to equal access to land, though only to a limited extent. By 2001, government policy recognised the need for joint registration between spouses for land acquired under the country's land reform programmes. By 2005, the arguments that were being advanced by the women's rights organisations that Section 23 of the Constitution, which allowed for discrimination on the basis of personal and customary law, was detrimental to women's right to be treated as equals in access to land, were gaining traction with the state. This led to an amendment to Section 23 (3) of the Constitution in 2005 through Constitutional Amendment Number 17 by inserting Section 23 (3a). Through this amendment, for the first time, the Constitution recognised the right of women to equality and non-discrimination in accessing agricultural land by outlawing discrimination on the basis of customary law in the allocation of resettlement land.

However, whilst the policy and legal documents were being changed to accommodate the issues raised by the women's rights organisations in their engagement with the state, there were no tangible efforts to translate the policy and legal changes into access to land for women. For example, despite government concessions on the need for joint registration of acquired land under the FTLRP, by 2012, government officials responsible for land redistribution and registration were not implementing the policy consistently or at all. Officers responsible for land allocation at local level indicated that whilst they had heard government 'talk' of allocating 20% of available land to women, such a position never went beyond announcements, usually by politicians at political gatherings. There was no implementation document to guide them during the actual land allocation process – and this was more than twelve years after the beginning of the FTLRP. Serious efforts by government to address this anomaly were only seen with the promulgation of SI 53/2014.

The engagement by the women's rights organisations with visible power focused purely on high-level visible power but failed to address other forms, levels and dimensions of power in the fast track land reform matrix. Respondents in both the rural areas and the farms knew very little about either ZWRCN or WLLG, although WLLG was specifically established to address women's land needs under the FTLRP. The women knew about ZWLA as a generalist women's rights organisation but had no specific knowledge of their work with regards to access to land by women. Mrs TM of Chidza farm knew of ZWLA and its work regarding women and girls' inheritance rights. This had led her to conclude that upon her death, all her eleven children, male and female, should somehow benefit from the land she had acquired under the programme, if they had an interest in farming. Men also knew about ZWLA and its women's rights' programmes, in particular those relating to divorce, maintenance and inheritance. Mr CM, a headmaster at a primary school, although not entirely agreeing with some of ZWLA's pronouncements, especially those relating to sharing of property upon divorce, agreed with their work in teaching women about their inheritance rights. Most of the information about the work of ZWLA reached the women and men that were interviewed through educational radio programmes and through radio news giving women valuable information on their general rights. Since then, ZWLA has started engaging specifically on women's land rights, including the capacity development of lawyers to litigate in the area, providing legal and rights literacy on the issue to rural women and traditional leaders and undertaking public interest litigation to challenge discrimination against women in access to fast track land.

6.4. A1 Women Engaging with Hidden and Invisible Power at the Local Farm and Family Level

The state stamped some form of power and authority over the land reform process the moment it made a decision to condone the farm invasions and take sides with the farm invaders. State structures at district and provincial level such as the district and provincial lands officers from the Ministry of Lands and Rural Resettlement, the Provincial Governors and the District and Provincial Administrators (DA/PA) from the Ministry of Local Government stepped in to 'regularise and rationalise' the process.

At this stage, the government encouraged people to stop the farm invasions and instead apply to government for land if they wanted land. Such calls were, however, largely ignored with the invaders expecting to be allocated land on the farms that they had occupied. This convenient chaos created fertile ground for the exercise of hidden power as murky local level power dynamics emerged at the farm level.

The A1 farmers in my research area were mostly affected by this state of affairs where decisions were made at the local farm level. The A2 farmers were less directly affected as decisions on land access were more centralised at national or provincial level and based on clearer (if not often followed) criteria. When they were followed, the criteria were beneficial to some women, particularly those in already empowered positions who were able to identify the power sources and engage with it at provincial and national level. Such empowered women included the educated, the resource endowed and the well-connected who were able to use their 'power within' to negotiate their access to land. There were fewer such women among the A1 farmers who relied on and followed available structures to try and access land.

Even with the government's apparent stamp of authority on the A1 farms, the reality was that local farm-level institutions and individuals ruled the day. In the absence of perceptible rules, it was their decisions that were usually rubber-stamped by the land officers and district administrators who would allocate land as per list of beneficiaries and attendant allocations agreed on at the farm level.

A1 women had to negotiate with the farm-level power, which included the war veterans and other mainly male leaders. In many instances they were happy to receive any land that came their way, given that women were regarded as followers of a process that was led by men. The hidden power of farm leaders triumphed over the visible state power on the farms. State level institutions were given directions by the local farm level leaders on how land allocations should be carried out and who would benefit from the land allocations, as well as the particular land that each identified person would receive.

Similarly, invisible power played a role in the land allocation patterns on the farms. The perception that women held of their inferior role in the occupations was ingrained in traditional and cultural attitudes towards them as lesser beings. As a result, the women were prepared to accept less valuable land because they saw men as superior and leading the process, so deserving of more and better land. Invisible power also played a role at the family level. This was seen in situations where women allowed land that was allocated to them to be registered in the names of their husbands and sons because traditionally a woman is not expected to own or control land, when there are men in the family.

Following court challenges by the white commercial farmers over the invasions and compulsory acquisition of land, the government instituted laws aimed at protecting existing farm invaders (Rural Land Occupiers (Protection from Eviction) Act [Chapter 20:26] and providing some guidance over future land acquisition processes. Amendments were made to the Land Acquisition Act [Chapter 20:10] and the Constitution through Constitutional Amendments Number 16 and 17. Essentially, these laws were to endorse the invasions and the compulsory land acquisition and set the tone and mode of compensation for improvements on the acquired land. Effectively the government concluded that the state would not pay compensation for the acquired land, which, they said, would be the responsibility of the colonial master Britain, with the Government of Zimbabwe only providing compensation for improvements made on the farms.

The power that was exercised by the state in this instance was visible in that it invoked the legislature and supposedly open decision-making processes to enact laws that governed the process. On the other hand, the power was negative in nature in that it was prescriptive and authoritarian, requiring compliance from those at whom it was directed (power over). History has shown that land laws have always served the interests of the dominant class (Mushunje, 2005:13). For women in Zimbabwe, the question that arises is whether the state through its exercise of visible power and legislative authority was able to provide clarity of process and purpose in their land acquisition efforts. The answer is 'no' in that for many women, the process remained unguided and unclear as no specific legal provisions were put in place to facilitate gender inclusive land reform. Moreover, the employment of visible power by the state was often countered by invisible power locally exercised. This reflects the reality for the citizen, who despite public law making and policy pronouncements, is unable to benefit from such laws due to local power dynamics.

6.5 A2 Individual Women Engaging with Visible Power at the local level

It was the empowered women who exercised their 'power within' and managed to engage with visible state power in a discernible way i.e. specifically those on the A2 sugar estates. This is not to say that women in A1 farms did not engage with visible power. Such engagement was, however, limited when compared to the women in A2 farms. The latter reported that the institutions, actors and structures with which they dealt in order to access A2 farms were discernible, targetable and identifiable although this was not always easy. This was because the spaces that were provided were limited in nature or inaccessible due to distance and structural barriers such as the self-importance of the actors involved, the political agenda and the political identity of the women farmers. Politics in its various manifestations was the hidden power that influenced the accessibility or otherwise of visible power.

Politically connected women found it easier to engage with visible state power and institutions compared to those who were not. Generally, however, the A2 women made efforts to identify and use available policies and institutions to acquire land. They were aware of which and what levels to engage with following 'invitations' into certain spaces by government as it called on qualifying citizens to apply for A2 farms. The results, however, were not always predictable as visible state power was often met by hidden or invisible power, and it sometimes proved more dominant. Consequently, the rights of women to access land as equals with men was often challenged by invisible power.

In many African societies, including Zimbabwe, women generally occupy subordinate positions that are entrenched through gender stereotyping and socialisation. This, in turn, makes it difficult for them to effectively engage with power and participate in decision-making processes. For example, economic handicaps make it difficult for women to make serious economic decisions. Without such power, women are disadvantaged in other aspects of life (Hutson, 2007:2) which again lead to their subordination. In the end, gender discrimination mutates into women's dispensability under a "development' which suppresses, excludes and devalues women' (Shiva, 2004: unpaginated). This exclusion is more evident in situations where the allocation of high value economic resources such as land is at the centre of the power relations. As a result, even though men with limited education, financial resources or political connections, faced similar challenges under the FTLRP, comparatively speaking, women remain more marginalised and excluded. This arises as a result of patriarchal power relations that lead to the domination of men over women – 'power over' – at various social, economic, cultural and political levels.

Although etymologically 'patriarchy' signified 'rule of fathers', its meaning has metamorphosed in contemporary society to include any powerful adult males including male bosses, leaders in society, in politics and in government, brothers, husbands, sons and uncles in the home and male community leaders, etc, in what has been called 'the men's league' or the 'men's house' (Mies, 1986:37, Chakona, 2011:13). Patriarchal society and the power it wields over women ultimately has the effect of control over them, and this includes the views that they hold about themselves, their capabilities and capacities and their rights and entitlements.

Under the FTLRP, in a general sense, women had to be content with accessing land as a basic resource which they could deploy for basic survival purposes and not for upward social and economic mobility. The latter was only possible if women were able to access prime, economically viable land; consider access to such land as a business opportunity; and had the necessary resources to fully and effectively utilise it as such. Women could harbour such ambitions if they were in possession of the requisite economic, political and social capital that would allow them to use it effectively. Access to high value land on the A2 farms was critical for women's economic empowerment.

6.6 War Veterans' Power Versus Women's Power

Table 4.1 in Chapter 4 shows that in both A1 and A2 allocations, the percentage access for women was 11,17%, an insignificant figure as women constitute 52% of the population of Zimbabwe (GoZ/UNDP Fast Facts, MDGs, Ndulo Undated: 194). Thus although ZANU-PF, GoZ, some researchers (e.g. Scoones et al., 2010, Hanlon et al., 2013), hailed the land reform programme as a successful empowerment model for indigenous Zimbabweans, the programme clearly failed to address gender inequalities thereby perpetuating the skewed gender-based power, land, property, social and economic relations in the country.

We should however note that women and the women's movement in Zimbabwe had not sat on the side-lines and observed the FTLRP. Women participated in the farm invasions, although in smaller numbers to men. Ironically, however, their lobbying of visible state power sometimes seemed to produce antithetical results as senior officials did not take their demands seriously. In February 2010, the then Women Affairs, Gender and Community Development Minister Olivia Muchena rejected calls by the Women's Coalition of Zimbabwe (WCoZ) for an urgent land audit to pave the way for a fresh farm redistribution programme that would address gender imbalances in land ownership. She was quoted as insisting that women's land needs had been met because government had a policy requiring that 20% of the redistributed land must be given to women, and that an 18% allocation threshold for women had since been met.

At that point (2010), the ZANU-PF government had consistently rejected calls for a land audit. Muchena stood with government, and as

Minister of Women Affairs, dismissed the women's movement, fellow women and their demands. This offers an example of hidden power at play: party politics implicitly dictated government responses to women's legitimate demands for land. The state could afford to ignore the women's voice and their power, because unlike the war veterans for example, they did not present any compelling threat to those in government or the political establishment.

6.7 Mobilising Women's Power and Neglecting them when success is achieved

In light of the disregard for women by the authorities, one must ask the following question::

> Would it have made a difference if women as a group had adopted a more militant approach to their demand for land, as opposed to lobbying and negotiating with power, in pursuit of a solution rooted in peace?

During the war of liberation both the nationalists and the settler governments used men's perceived inborn capacity for violence to recruit them for armed combat while women were recruited and mobilised as providers of care and comfort (Nhongo-Simbanegavi, 2000:14). This also included provision of food to the fighters, caring for the wounded and providing sexual services to the fighters on the battlefront, in the villages and in the training camps. The result was that in independent Zimbabwe, the men who were at the frontline were given hero status as the liberators of the country which had attendant economic, social and political benefits whilst the women who provided non-combat but essential services were seen as non-essential, not recognised and indeed often regarded as prostitutes (Chogugudza, Undated:34, Zimbabwe Women Writers, 2000)

During the liberation struggle, women also sustained the struggle on the 'home front' by ensuring that while the men were away, homes were kept and maintained, children were looked after, agricultural production in the rural areas continued and that the guerrillas were fed, clothed and taken care of (see Staunton, 1990). A woman with a gun in her hands and a baby on her back was the standard image by which a link was made between national liberation and women's liberation (Mies, 1986: 175, Lyons, 2004: xix) by showing the dexterity of women and their capabilities as both mothers and liberation war fighters. But soon after the war, men and the state assumed political power and women were forced to retreat into their 'natural' roles because their men were once again available to take up 'their roles' and power as national leaders and heads of families. For example, in 1980, the Government of Zimbabwe could not provide enough wage labour to the ex-guerrillas resulting in it giving the available jobs to men rather than women (Mies, 1986: 196). Women could only benefit once the men were satisfied.

Women are treated before and after elections in the same way. They play their part as campaign leaders, party supporters and voters while the politicians make promises. 'Women's projects' spring up everywhere, only to be abandoned as soon as the election is over. The 2013 election was a critical one for the major political parties that were involved and as usual, women were men's 'political fodder' and were encouraged to vote for the parties on the promise of gender equality and the promotion of women's rights. The parties' election manifestos had clear gender equality clauses that were designed to get the women's attention. The ZANU-PF manifesto stated in part that:

> Inspired by the heroism of Mbuya Nehanda against colonialism and the historical fact that women fought side by side with their male counterparts during the liberation struggle, the goal of gender equality is profoundly embedded in the Zimbabwean mind-set. It is for this reason that every ZANU PF policy seeks gender equality as an aspiration of the liberation struggle. ZANU PF has raised the status of women by championing gender equality through laws, empowerment programmes and promotion of women in sectors and positions previously held by men only. Examples include a woman Vice President since 2005, female judges, and pilots to mention a few. The party will consolidate programmes to economically empower women, build strong families and develop [co]mmunities where men and women, boys and girls are equal partners and beneficiaries in development. (ZANU PF, Elections Manifesto, 2013: 21).

The MDC-T's election manifesto was more to the point in relation to women and access to land and stated that the party would:

> Implement a fair and equitable land policy to cultivate an efficient, just and people driven agro-economy by [ensuring] equitable access

to land for all irrespective [of] race or *gender* [emphasis mine] (MDC, Election Manifesto, 2013: 13).

In other words, both political parties recognised that women were a decisive constituency in influencing their election success. In addition, women and women's issues were central to the constitution-making discussions and the adoption of the 2013 Constitution before the elections later in the year. Concessions were made on all sides of the political divide, including those relating to women's land rights. However even with these rights entrenched in the Constitution, unless such provisions are positively implemented, they will be meaningless and only remembered when the next election approaches. Yet, arguably, women could use their 'power with', to mobilise and withdraw their vote and party support if their land needs continue to be unmet. In my view, patriarchal state and political power will only yield to women's power if it effectively threatens their own positions as leaders. Currently, the state, political parties and male leaders can afford to disregard women and their rights as their power is assumed to be negligible. But, women could collectively use their 'power with' to withdraw their support of political parties in order to achieve a common goal like access to land.

When I went into the field in March 2014, it was just seven months after the country's general elections, held on the 31 July 2013. It was clear that the land issue was a major campaign point for the two main political parties, ZANU-PF and MDC-T during the election period. Beneficiaries of the FTLRP supported the party in return for retaining the land allocated to them. There was no backlash from the women who failed to acquire land, who could have withdrawn their support for ZANU-PF and voted for the MDC-T, which was promising a land audit and the implementation of a programme that would benefit many more citizens. Access to land failed to act as a rallying point for women; party allegiances proved more important than their land needs or women's rights and a women's issues one.

6.8 Access Patterns and Access Challenges as Indicators of Prevailing Power Relations

The land access patterns identified during research were a reflection of the prevailing power issues at play during the FTLRP. Women who accessed land on the A1 farms were not necessarily content with the land that they were given but they lacked the necessary 'power within' to engage with the processes that would have enabled them to access land on the high-value A2 farms. Similarly, some women in the communal areas were also desirous of acquiring land either in A1 or A2 farms but were in an even more invidious position in relation to their capacity and power to engage with the relevant processes. Box 6.1 details some of the reasons why women in the A1 allocations failed to access A2 plots and why those in the communal areas failed to access land despite their need for it.

Box 6.1: Reasons provided by women on why those on A1 farms failed to access A2 farms and why others completely failed to access land under the FTLRP

Reasons why women in A1 farms failed to access land in A2 farms

Lack of information on processes to be followed
- Lack of resources to fulfil resource capacity requirements, a condition for accessing A2 farms
- No political connections to facilitate access to high value A2 plots
- Complicated application procedures requiring high levels of education and resources to hire technical expertise to draft business plans where they were required.

Reasons why some women completely failed to access land despite their wish to access land
- Lack of information on processes to be followed
- Lack of resources to clear plots, construct new homes and invest in production on the new farms
- Fear of violence on the farms
- Viewed the ability to benefit as linked being to party affiliation and political connections, and therefore did not try these being without such connections
- Complicated application procedures for A2 farm applications
- Old age
- Gender roles inhibiting participation (for example looking after children and the home whilst the men went out looking for land)

Box 6.1 relates to women who accessed land in A1 farms and those in communal areas who failed to access land. Both categories of women were marginalised and disempowered in various social, economic and political spheres. Their challenges – lack of information, lack of resources and political influence and know-how – were common to women on both A1 farms and in the communal areas, though issues of age and fear of violence mostly affected the women in the communal areas who completely failed to access land.

Women's heterogeneity denotes that they are differently impacted by similar issues and comparable challenges. Although 'women' as a category provides a convenient catch-all term, 'women' like the concept of 'property' should be subjected to analytical scrutiny (Hirschon, 1984:3) in order to understand the situation that each woman, and different categories of women, find themselves in. Power and power relations provide a category of analysis that illuminates the differences between (categories of) women and how they respond to issues and challenges. In Chapter 4, I examined the manner in which women on A2 farms engaged with and challenged dominant power as they sought to carve a place for themselves in the high value A2 sugar-cane farms. Women on the A1 farms and communal areas did not benefit as they had hoped from the FTLRP, revealing that they were differently placed in relation to the dominant power relations at play. This section will therefore seek to analyse how power and power relations affected this category of women and the differences in responses when compared to the A2 women beneficiaries.

6.8.1 Lack of Information on Processes to be Followed

Both women in the A1 resettlement allocations, who wanted but failed to access A2 farms and those in communal areas who completely failed to access land cited lack of information about the programme and the processes to be followed as a reason for their failure. Yet to a disinterested onlooker information on the FTLRP in Zimbabwe was abundant, judging by the television and print media coverage that the issue received both nationally and internationally. However, the available information and the manner in which it was packaged and conveyed was not appropriate in helping women participate and make informed decisions. Effectively, therefore, women (particularly those in communal areas) had no useful material to help them with the process.

This meant that they did not have the necessary 'power within' to engage with visible power. This led to their exclusion from the land reform exercise despite their apparent need to benefit from it. It is often said 'Information is power' and without it, women, in this case, were vulnerable. Moreover, information on the FTLRP was not transmitted to citizens through formal government channels but was often appropriated by local strongmen such as war veterans and traditional leaders and thus rarely either consistent or clear. Respondents identified their main sources of information on the programme, including farms that could be targeted for invasion as:

i. Family members
ii. The local war veteran and
iii. Fellow villagers.

These in their turn indicated that they had received the information from 'other people' or from media reports showing how people were on a mission to reclaim their 'ancestral land'. Additionally, some of the local strongmen with information used it sparingly and strategically to benefit their kith and kin first before they transmitted it to people beyond their immediate family and friends. The following comments from interviewees exemplify such practices:

Ms AS – Musvovi Communal Lands:

The war veterans in this village simply went to invade the farms first and came back later to take their friends and relatives. That is how some of the people in our village managed to get land.

Mr DB – Bejani Village, Shindi Communal Lands:

We hear that war veterans got bigger plots compared to other people and hoarded them. They would then allocate the land to other people of their choice. In our area, there is no war veteran so there was no one to lead us to the farms and in the land invasion process. No one in the village knew where to go or how to go about the process. As a result, we didn't get a chance to also get land. If you know how it's being done, please tell us so that we can also go and get land [referring to me].

The reality is that people in the communal areas did not have the requisite information on the FTLRP, a lacuna that affected both men and women in the communal areas. Nonetheless, the situation was mitigated for the men who socialised and met other people outside their homes and villages. The townships, in particular, were often points of convergence and sources of information for rural men who spent considerable time at these centres drinking beer, socialising or merely relaxing. Here a newspaper might be passed on and read by many men at the township throughout the day. As custodians of information on the FTLRP, the men would recount the news to their wives, mothers and sisters when they returned home. Even then, such information rarely provided details about how land could be accessed. More often it was about the 'progress' of the farm invasions in different parts of the country or what the senior political figures were saying about the situation. Empowerment and the rhetoric of anti-colonialism provided the focus, and propaganda about the need to remain patriotic and support President Robert Mugabe and ZANU-PF. In addition, state television provided constant jingles reminding people to stay resolute. Songs such as *'Rambai Makashinga'* and *'Hondo Yeminda'* were a constant feature, none of which helped women to understand and participate in the programme.

Properly packaged and properly conveyed information was essential for women's participation and inclusion in the FTLRP, yet it was lacking. Indeed, the United Nations (Rio) Declaration on Environment and Development, urges state parties to ensure public awareness and citizen participation in decision-making processes by ensuring that appropriate access to information is made widely available.

These undertakings have been adopted at the African Union, SADC and at national level in Zimbabwe through legislation such as the Environmental Management Act [Chapter 20:27]. Thus the government should have ensured that information on the FTLRP was properly conveyed through reliable channels to enable the marginalised to access and act on that information. The involvement of local government officials in rural areas where the availability of media is limited was critical if information about the FTLRP was to be properly conveyed to everyone in the rural areas, including women. The absence of information effectively disempowered rural women.

6.8.2 Lack of Resources

A second common challenge for women on the A1 farms and those in communal areas inhibiting their effective participation in the FTLRP was lack of resources. For the former, who wanted but failed to access land in the A2 farms, they required resources to demonstrate that they had the means to utilise an A2 farm and engage experts in the development of a business plan, if they could not do it on their own. A business plan was a requirement for one to access A2 land, though not necessarily followed in all cases. Hanlon, et al., note in this regards that:

> The Ministry placed advertisements in the main national newspapers inviting people to apply, and application forms required a business plan setting out cash flow and budgets as well as specifying the applicant's income, property, experience, qualifications, and training. Applicants were required to have their own resources for farming without government support. Special consideration was given to war veterans, war collaborators, ex-detainees, and women. (Hanlon, et al., 2013:85).

This observation was confirmed by the Masvingo PA, who stated that:

> In order to access an A2 farm, one had to show capacity to farm and the level of capacity would also impact on whether one would get a ranch or a commercial cropping farm. Capacity was determined by relevant educational qualifications, financial and other capital resources amongst other things. This was also one of the reasons why less women benefitted in the A2 farms because not many of them could meet these requirements and criteria for allocation

However, even though government as confirmed by the PA was acutely aware of the challenges faced by women in relation to these requirements, there was no deliberate effort to ensure that they were assisted to correct their obvious disadvantages. Women in the communal areas lacked basic resources for simple actions to assist them to get established on the new farms i.e. to clear land, plough it, build homes and buy inputs necessary to initiate their farming activities. The net effect in the context of the FTLRP was to alienate the land users and food producers from the land, given that women are the workers of the land and produce food for families and nations.

Utete (2003) highlighted the gender disparities in access to land under the FTLRP and the effect on gender equality, women's empowerment and the fight against the feminisation of poverty amongst the rural women in Zimbabwe. The Utete Commission emphasised the need to recognise the 'historically diverse and pivotal role of women in all aspects of agriculture in the communal lands and the need to strike an overall gender balance' in the agricultural sector by implementing measures that would ensure equity in, and the effectiveness of, the agrarian reform in the country (Utete, 2003:6). In addition, the report stressed the need 'to ensure the survival and stability of the growing number of families in rural areas headed by women' (Utete, 2003:6) It further pointed out that children were also increasingly heading households as a result of the devastation of communities by the HIV and AIDS pandemic. The Commission acknowledged the low levels of access by women in the FTLRTP at only 18%, but argued that the agrarian reform was a significant vehicle for economically empowering women (Utete, 2003: 6).

A lack of resources further entrenches women's lack of autonomy and inability to negotiate and participate in decision-making in the home, in the community and at the national level, leading to unfavourable decisions and outcomes for them. Education was also a critical resource that many women lacked. With education, it would have been easier for the women to compile the requisite applications. The 'Human Capital Theory' asserts that education creates skills, which facilitate higher levels of productivity' amongst the people that have them in comparison with those who do not (Oxaal, 1997:3). But it has also been proved that in developing countries, women typically receive less education than men. Although Zimbabwe has one of the highest literacy rates in Africa at 97.9% for women and 96.9% for men in 2019 (Zimstat, 2019), , this could not have had a significant impact on women's ability to negotiate their land rights under the FTLRP, especially if one considers what this literacy means. Zimstat, Zimbabwe's official statistical agency defines literacy as

> The ability to read and write, with understanding, a simple statement related to one's daily life. It involves a continuum of reading skill and often includes basic arithmetic skills (numeracy). In Zimbabwe, persons aged 15 years and above and have completed at least grade three of primary education are considered to be literate. (Zimstat, 2019:26).

A Grade 3 primary education would not have helped in the application process for the A2 farm allocations, because the process was complicated. A higher level of education was necessary and yet the higher the educational qualification level, the fewer women there are (especially in the rural areas). According to Zimstat in 2012, 'school enrolment from primary level up to Form 3 showed gender parity… however, from Form 4 to tertiary level, enrolment was still in favour of males' (Zimstat 2012: 29). From 2017 however, Zimstat statistics show that women are now ahead of males post-O-Level with 52% of all university entrants being female (Zimstat 2019: 43). Currently, over 70% of Level One law students at the University of Zimbabwe are female.[1] However, these developments were noticeable many years after the FTLRP, too late for this to impact positively on women. Moreover, it takes time for gains to permeate society and without access to the relevant information, literacy levels on their own are unlikely to help women in meaningful ways.

Zimstat notes that 'In the age groups below 45 years, there is gender parity in literacy. However, in older age groups, literacy is generally higher in men than in women' (Zimstat, 2012:24). In 2000, the United Nations estimated that 60% of Zimbabwean women were illiterate (UN, 2000 quoted in Mushunje 2005:39) with women in the rural areas being the most disadvantaged and women generally leaving school earlier than their male counterparts (Mushunje, 2005:39). In my research area, of the nineteen female interviewees in control of the land they occupied (single, widowed, allocated in own right) only six (13.3%) were below the age of 45. In other words, the majority of people who made an effort to access land were in the older age group, i.e. with more limited education. As such, they were disadvantaged in their interaction with the land reform process in the high value A2 allocations due to their limited educational levels.

The mere act of occupying land also required resources especially in relation to farms that were far away from one's normal place of abode. Money was required for transport and food amongst other necessities as people camped on the farms. Distant occupations were therefore difficult without financial resources. As a result, many of the distant land occupiers were men who were occupying on their own behalf or as proxies of the elite who for one reason or another were not prepared to camp on the farms as land invaders (Matondi, 2012:23).

Respondents showed that whilst the actual land was presented as a free commodity that was there for the taking, in reality the invaders

---

[1] As of 2020, and according to the Director of SEARCWL, Professor Julie Stewart.

were required to contribute resources, in particular money for various issues on the farms as detailed below by one of the respondents. The contributions were arbitrarily set by the war veterans and other leaders on the farms and there was no accounting afterwards. One was required to pay in order to remain part of the programme or any particular group camping on the farms. The power that the war veterans and farm leaders had over the other occupants meant that the latter were coerced into making the contributions or risked losing their land or not being allocated any in situations where the parcelling out had not yet taken place. Mrs JC from the Musvovi Communal Lands recounted the problem of lack of resources and the coercive money collection methods thus:

> The other problem was that whilst the farms were on the face of it being given for free, people were required to contribute money towards a lot of things, for example for the war veterans and other leaders to go to the government ministries in Masvingo to process the papers. If there were visitors especially people from government ministries in Masvingo or the 'Chief' , people would be asked to contribute towards their food, transport or a gift. The war veterans were the ones who commandeered everything and led the collection of contributions. Those who failed to pay the money were pushed out and those who paid stayed in. At the end of the day therefore your money talked.

This meant that without resources, remaining on the farms, which had been invaded, was difficult, and one of the reasons why women were eventually elbowed out.

The issue of resources continued to plague women even after they had settled on the farms as access to resources determined their productivity and their capacity to retain the land they had been allocated. For example, during fieldwork on the Hippo Valley Estates, it was reported that productivity on A2 farms was a pre-requisite for obtaining a 99-year lease. This tenure system was considered as optimal since it enabled loans from banks and other credit providers for farm inputs, etc. Failure to get 99-year leases due to lack of resources and the attendant low productivity therefore showed the disadvantages that women continued to face on the farms.

6.9 The Role of Politics, Political Power and Political Relations

The role of politics and the fact that the FTLRP was a political process and power game cannot be over-emphasised. Moyo stresses this point:

> It makes no sense however, to pretend that the land question is not a political issue, and that it should only be addressed following purely economic logic… the land issue is a political issue, which has to be addressed with full cognisance of the political problems it invokes (Moyo, 1995: 17).

Thus, the politics of the day played a key role in determining how the FTLRP was implemented and eventually who benefited and how. Initially, the political schemes around the FTLRP centred purely on power games, and ensuring an electoral win for ZANU-PF in the 2000 elections. (As mentioned above, their position had been threatened first by the strikes of 1997, then by the loss of the referendum on the constitution, and, finally, by the rise of an opposition party, which appeared very popular.) However, over time, the politics of patronage and reward, political party affiliation, social and blood relationships determined who the beneficiaries were. Although the government consistently denied that access to land was done along partisan political lines and that all citizens were eligible, the reality, as evidenced by other researchers, tells a different story. Political power, whether personally held or by proxy or association, was in reality and in the public perception one of the major (but not sole) determining factors as to whether one accessed land or not. As Matondi posits:

> Land allocation under the FTLRP was not expected to benefit everyone because the land acquired was limited… this meant that a specific number of people could benefit, and, naturally, some people would not benefit. In a context in which land as a resource was limited and there were many people competing for access, it meant allocation became a political act of balancing multiple interests. Some politicians sought to influence land allocation as a basis for building their support base (Matondi, 2012:52).

In addition, the same author states that there is no doubt that many people who wanted land used the political approach to acquire it and that there was nothing extraordinary about this (Ibid, 74). Despite this reality, Matondi and other researchers (Scoones et al., 2010, Moyo and Yeros, 2005) downplay the impact of this political approach by arguing that at the end of the day it was the ordinary person and not the so-called 'cronies' that benefitted. My argument is different: it is that political power and connections, political influences and relationships had an impact on how the marginalised, in particular women, related to and approached the land reform programme. It impacted on how they made decisions on whether or not to participate and if they were to do so, the best political strategy they should adopt in order to benefit from the programme. Those with political affiliations leant on them whilst those without, were forced to fake them in order to be accepted as beneficiaries. At the end of the day, we must ask if the ordinary person did benefit, at what cost?

Box 6.2 below shows how some respondents used their political affiliations to negotiate access to land.

Box 6.2 Examples of how women in my research area benefitted from political connections or relationships and personal political affiliations to ZANU-PF and Senior ZANU-PF officials

Mrs PC (A1 Allocation): She was assisted to get a 32-hectare plot in Lothian Farm by her late husband's younger brother Major General C who was a war veteran and a senior army officer. Major General C took Mrs PC to the farm and introduced her to the war veteran (Mr FZ) who was in charge of the occupations on that particular farm. The war veteran promised to allocate a piece of land to Mrs PC once the allocations started and encouraged Mrs PC to camp on the farm with the other invaders. Mrs PC did so and was allocated her plot when the time for allocations came.

Mrs M9 (A2 Allocation): She was assisted by her brother-in-law, a Major General who was a senior army officer and at one time was a ZANU-PF MP in Bikita District, to obtain a plot on the sugar estates, as he also did.

Mrs RM 2 (A1 Allocation): She inherited the farm from her husband who was a war veteran who died a few years after they had settled on the farm. (The farm was still registered in her late husband's name at the time of my research.)

Mrs C (A2 Allocation): A senior ZANU-PF official in Masvingo Province, she was the Provincial Women's League Treasurer and the Provincial Chairperson of the Zimbabwe War Collaborators Association, a ZANU-PF affiliated organisation. She had direct access to the Provincial Governor, a key actor in the allocation of A2 farms as the chairperson of the Provincial Lands Committee.

The over-representation of politically connected individuals compared to other citizens on the farms gave credence to perceptions that access to land under the FTLRP was to a large extent politically determined. As such, space for participation by non-affiliated individuals, in particular women, was compromised despite the apparently open invitations for people to participate in the programme. Consequently, sometimes potential participants to the programme, who were not members of ZANU-PF, played the political card and claimed affiliation. During an FGD at Nuanetsi Ranch in September 2010, participants outdid each other in publicly praising and thanking the then President of Zimbabwe, Robert Mugabe for giving them land. It was clear that the public nature of the discussions necessitated that people publicly proclaim their allegiance and publicly acknowledge the person or entity they attributed their land acquisition to, lest they be mistaken for belonging to the opposition or be accused of not being grateful to President Mugabe and ZANU-PF. Such tags could lead to one being 'chucked out' of the farms by the war veterans, traditional leaders or other local strongmen. Similar praise-singing was not necessarily present during individual interviews held in private. The public display of allegiance was simply a strategy against displacement.

As stated above, some researchers have argued that ordinary people and ordinary women benefitted from the FTLRP as compared to the so-called 'cronies' or elites (Scoones, 2010, Mutopo, 2011). Mutopo for example argues that:

> The fast track presented a life opportunity for most women that had never happened in the history of land relations in Zimbabwe. In comparison to the land resettlement programme in the 1980s and 1990s, the number of women gaining access to land has escalated under fast track, which may be attributed to changes in the way the societies are evolving (Mutopo, 2011:1023).

Whilst, I acknowledge that more women acquired land under the FTLRP than they did in the early post-independence land reform programme (5% according to Hanlon, et al., 2013) and indeed during the colonial era, this analysis fails to acknowledge that women generally still acquired a fraction of the available land and that 'ordinary' women often acquired 'left-over' land. It is, however, my contention that there is no reason why this state of affairs should be perpetuated, especially following a period of radical reform such as the FTLRP whose mission was to dismantle the *status quo* and usher in a new era of empowerment for the marginalised.

The findings in my research area mirror those of Matondi (2012:185) in Mazowe District where ordinary women did indeed receive land but usually marginal land, that is after the men and the elite women (often those with political affiliations) were satisfied with their own allocations. In many instances, 'ordinary' women came on the scene at a later stage. On the sugar-cane estates in Hippo Valley, the names of the female beneficiaries sounded like a 'who is who' in the Masvingo Provincial ZANU-PF party structures including political leaders, former MPs, cabinet ministers, wives, daughters, sisters and sisters-in-law of high-ranking party and military officers as well as senior civil servants. Political affiliation, political power and access to sources of power and decision-makers had a significant bearing on access to land by women. Yet it has been emphasised that women in politics or with political affiliations are comparatively few, a point that was confirmed by the Masvingo PA.[2] Statistics also show that the level of participation by women in national level politics is also very limited: see Table 6.1, which shows the level of representation of women in Parliament between 1980 and 2005.

Table 6.1: Women's participation in legislative bodies in Zimbabwe from 1980 to 2005

	1980-84	1985-90	1990-95	1995-00	2000-05
House of Assembly: Total	100	100	150	150	150
Men	91	92	129	128	136
Women	9	8	21	22	14
% Women	9	8	14	14.1	9.3

Source: Gaidzanwa R, 2004, p. 45

During the years 2000-05, the peak period of the FTLRP, the rate of women's representation in Parliament dropped from a high of 14.1% in the period 1995-2000 to only 9.3%. While the mere presence of women

---

2   The PA confirmed that political party politics played a role in the A2 land allocation process and that fewer women actively participated in politics when compared to men, which explained their marginalisation in the land allocation process.

in Parliament or other national decision-making bodies does not directly or necessarily correlate with the creation or implementation of gender sensitive laws and policies, their contribution both qualitatively and quantitatively can still play a role in influencing the formulation and interpretation of gender sensitive laws and policies (Mushunje, 2005:33). Limited female representation often filters down to other aspects of women's rights, in this case the right to land due to the influence that politics, political affiliation and often outright political patronage can play in determining access to resources. The Masvingo PA confirmed this causal connection between politics and access to land for women during an interview in September 2010 when he said 'In many cases, business and political leaders monopolised access to land under the programme, and there are not many women in those circles.'[3]

We can conclude, however, that politics and political power was a key determinant in women's ability to negotiate access to land for themselves. Decisions regarding their access to land were often made at the national or provincial level following negotiations that took place behind the scenes. However, because not many women had access to such power, this was reflected by low levels of access to land, especially in A2 farms. Ordinary women often had to use their ingenuity to create spaces for participation for themselves in the FTLRP by feigning ZANU-PF affiliation and participating in ZANU-PF activities. Faking such affiliation often continued well after someone had been allocated land because the threat of eviction for lack of allegiance remained present.

6.10 Old Age[4]

Old age is associated with a number of challenges, amongst them limited access to resources although the elderly are most in need of them. Often there is an assumption that the elderly do not need certain services or resources because they cannot work the land. Moreover, their age makes it difficult for them to engage with processes or interact with decision-makers resulting in them being side-lined. In relation to land under the FTLRP, there was no policy targeting the elderly as beneficiaries.

---

3   During an interview with the PA at his offices in Masvingo on 6 September 2010.
4   The Constitution of Zimbabwe regards an elderly person as someone above the age of 70 whilst HelpAge International regards a person over the age of 60 as elderly and in need of special treatment and attention. I have used the 60 years in this research to regard a person as elderly in line with international standards.

Therefore, elderly women faced intersectional discrimination: as women and because of their age. In addition, the lack of infrastructure, resources, proper implementation plans and the violence associated with the programme were equally significant reasons for the failure or inability of elderly women to participate in the FTLRP. Easily elbowed out, they could not compete without government assistance and specially targeted allocation of land. Yet older women have borne the burden of looking after grandchildren following the death of their fathers and mothers in a generation that was heavily impacted by HIV and AIDS.[5] In Zimbabwe as in other Africa countries, it is estimated that:

> … 60% of orphaned children live in grandparent headed households. It is often older women who provide this care: households headed by older women are twice as likely to include orphans as those headed by older men. (HelpAge International, 2008:5).

The elderly are forced to shoulder such responsibilities without the requisite resources. Moreover, although they were prioritised in the allocation of farming inputs such as fertilisers and seed, low-value resources, they are not prioritised for high value resources such as farming implements, tractors and combine harvesters, which were all distributed under the various government programmes to capitalise the agricultural sector. In both the communal areas and new resettlement farms, such high value resources were mostly allocated to senior ZANU-PF party members, local leaders and elites such as traditional leaders, war veterans, business people and ZANU-PF councillors. In my research area, both older women on the new farms and those in the communal areas who failed to access land under the FTLRP were looking after grandchildren and, in many instances, were struggling to obtain food and other resources for their upkeep.

Government policies and programmes should therefore pay special attention to older women, the majority of whom live in rural areas – women constitute 52% of the rural population (Zimstat, 2019). The mainstay of the rural economy is agriculture and older women continue to work in the fields to sustain themselves and their families, including grandchildren, even in very advanced age. The agrarian reform, which

---

5 In 2001, UNAIDS reported HIV/AIDS prevalence rates of 33.7% (See Joint United Nations Programme on AIDS. Report on the Global HIV/AIDS Epidemic. Geneva: UNAIDS, 2002).

sought to transform the rural economy, therefore left elderly women vulnerable by not providing them with land. Yet their livelihoods are land dependent and the traditional social structures that used to support the elderly have largely disintegrated. Kollapan notes that:

> While in traditional African societies older persons were generally supported and cared for by their children or extended family, the changing societal dynamics brought about by among other factors, globalisation, urbanisation and the HIV/AIDS pandemic has impacted negatively on the cohesion of the family and its ability to create a nurturing and enabling environment for the protection of older persons. Under these circumstances there is clearly a need for increased state intervention in support of the elderly based on universal human rights norms and standards. (Kollapan, 2008:1).

State intervention therefore was and remains an imperative in the country's land reform agenda, bearing in mind that age discrimination affects women more than men, and that the older women lack the power and capacity to negotiate access to land without the assistance of the state. The human rights dispensation that has been ushered in by the 2013 Constitution bodes well for creating and implementing frameworks for the protection of the rights of the elderly in access to land, especially considering that this is the first time in the history of the country that the rights of the elderly have been enshrined in this document.[6]

6.11 The Family as a Locus for Power Contestations

Invisible power in the FTLRP was more dominant at family and community level, with women often impaired in their land access efforts by contestations around culture, religion, tradition and societal expectations on the roles and 'acceptable' behaviour of women. As such, 'the land had its owners'[7] and the owners were men who were also leaders in the community and in the home. It has been argued that:

> Women's struggles for human rights often position them in opposition to family and social networks where their roles and rights have been defined; however, because of the sanctity of the family,

---

6   Sec 21 and sec 82.
7   P. Kameri-Mbote's article 'The land has its owners: Gender issues in land tenure in land tenure under customary law in Kenya' confirms the perception that in African society, land is regarded as a male resource and not one to be owned by women.

they often choose not to seek empowerment and freedom which sets them against their kin [and family]. (Fox, Undated, Unpaginated).

As a result, the family can play a negative role towards the internalisation of female powerlessness. Does this therefore mean that the family is inimical to women's empowerment? In many instances and situations, yes, it is; but this can be changed, as the family is the place where individuals can learn the importance of the rights of all members as individuals and as members of a community in particular and society as a whole. The family is also the unit where love and care should be nurtured and where values that promote love and respect can be imparted. As Coomaraswamy (1994: 52-53) has noted 'The law should protect and privilege that kind of family and no other'. The reality however is that the standard family is one that promotes patriarchy and the rule of men over women. The public face of men is that of heads of family and breadwinners, even when in reality the bread is being put on the table by the women of the family. For example, in Zimbabwe's agricultural economy, it is the women who work the land to ensure that families are fed and when there is a surplus for sale to meet other family needs such as hospital bills, education and clothing amongst others. Yet, at the end of the day, their labour and the output from the farms is appropriated by the men, and the women are expected to accept that state of affairs.[8]

As such, my fieldwork evinced that if married women played a role in the acquisition of land, the credit was supposed to go to the husband by ensuring that the acquired land was registered in his name. This ensured that power and control remained in the hands of the husband not the wife or wives, which would have resulted in the emasculation of male power. That outward display of power through ownership was primarily used as a signifier to other men on the farms and within the wider communities such as the communal areas where they originated. Phrases such as *'anogara pamunda wemukadzi'*,[9] were often used by men during my fieldwork to describe other men, whether married or not, who were living on farms that had been registered in the names of their wives

---

8   As highlighted above in this book, a woman respondent described how the GMB account was in her husband's name despite the fact that she was the one farming the land whilst her husband held a regular job in Masvingo.

9   When translated from Shona to English, this means that 'he is living on a woman's farm'.

or female partners. This implied that such men were not men enough in that the powerful person within their relationships was the woman, as she was the one who 'owned' the land. Johnson has described this effect of power and patriarchy vividly when he posited that:

> The cycle of control and fear that drives patriarchy has more to do with relations amongst men than with women, for it is men who control men's standing as men. With few exceptions, men look to other men – not women – to affirm their manhood. (Johnson, 1997:56)

He further states that men use women as badges of success, as they enhance their status before other men, signifying that they are the authority over such women. In this regard:

> People routinely compliment a man married to a beautiful woman, for example, not because he had a hand in making her beautiful but because he has proprietary rights of access to her. In contrast, people are much less likely to compliment a man whose wife is financially successful – especially if she earns more than he does – because this threatens rather than enhances his status as a real man. (Johnson, 1997:60)

A man's underlying feelings of being threatened by a woman's economic power and access to resources lie at the heart of the need for power, control and dominance (Gordon, 1996:105). Men influence and determine the behaviour of other men in a culture and social environment that glorifies validation and approval from other men in relation to their masculinity, power and control over women and resources. Though invisible, these social and cultural elements are inherently powerful and ubiquitous, commanding compliance from both men and women, especially at the family and community level.

It is this power that directly or indirectly pressurised women to register land that they had acquired in their own right in a husband's or son's name; the men gladly accepting or demanding to have that land registered in their names.[10] The woman agreed or even 'offered' to register the land in the husband's name because social pressure has led her to believe that she could not have land when the husband did not have any, and that failure to register land in the man's name would raise his ire. For

---
10 See for example the case of some of my respondents referred to above.

the man, the issue was that it was demeaning if his wife outmanoeuvred him that is if she managed to acquire land ahead of him as the husband and the 'breadwinner'. The resultant contestations are a manifestation of the struggle for power and control within the household. These often spill into the community with a spirited fight by the man that shows other men within the community that he is still in control within his household, even if the reality is otherwise. But do men in general and those responsible for policy and programme implementation at government level understand these dynamics enough to detect the nuances and ensure that in the end, women are not unnecessarily prejudiced by having their 'bread taken away from their mouths'.

One of my male respondents Mr FZ had a biblical justification for this state of affairs. He did not see anything wrong with women 'offering' to have land that they have acquired registered in their husbands' names because 'the Bible never gives the responsibility to feed families to women'. To him, therefore, having the farm registered in the name of the husband was only 'following God's Constitution'[11] and giving men their rightful positions as required by the Bible.

A worrying finding was that even government officials had a superficial approach to the issue of women 'offering' to register land in the husband's name. Once a woman made this 'offer', the government officials responsible for implementing the FTLRP would not interrogate the issue but would be relieved to grant the woman 'her wish'. Mr DM, an official in the Ministry of Lands and Rural Resettlement in Masvingo had this to say:

> If a woman who has acquired land offers to register the land in the name of the husband, which they normally do, we carry out her wish. It's only in situations where the husband is forcing the woman to register the land in his name and the wife is not willing to do so that we intervene to make sure that the woman's rights are protected.[12]

The protection that was accorded to women was therefore not adequate under the circumstances as what was manifested as willingness

---

11 Terms borrowed by author from P. Kameri-Mbote, P. and J.A. Oduor's 'Following God's Constitution: The gender dimensions in the Ogiek Claim to Mau Land' in Hellum, A. et al. (2007) *Human rights, plural legalities and gendered realities: Paths are made by walking.*

12 Interview held on 10 February 2012 in Masvingo.

to register land in the husband's name was not always what it appeared to be. In many instances, women lack the 'power within' to fight the invisible power and the invisible pressures that come from customary, community and religious norms and expectations of a married woman.

6.15 Conclusion

Power in its various dimensions, at various levels and in different spaces played a critical role in determining access to land by women under the FTLRP. Physical power in the form of the pervasive violence that accompanied the farm invasions had the effect of closing out spaces for participation in the programme for women. It was visible power that determined the policies that were made regarding the FTLRP from the national to the international level. Hidden power, however, often determined whether or not the policies were implemented, with institutions outside formal state authority ruling the day at the local level.

Invisible power, on the other hand, played on the women's minds, forcing them to internalise beliefs, customs and practices that led to their subordination and exploitation by men in the home, in the community and even at the state level. Women's organisations sought to engage with visible state power in order to change the fortunes of fellow women under the programme. But the failure to translate this engagement into empowerment or 'power to' for the women meant that the local women lacked the 'power with' or 'power within' to engage with the system and benefit from the programme. In conclusion, the power dynamics under the FTLRP weighed heavily against women, leading to limited access to land compared to men.

7

Conclusion

7.1 Introduction

The objective of any reorganisation or reform process is to bring about change. In the case of the FTRLP, change was to be achieved through redistributing land more equitably and ensuring access for those who had been disadvantaged by previous discriminatory practices, laws and policies. At the initiation of the programme, women had suffered discrimination in access to land for over a century, spanning both the colonial and post-colonial periods. The colonial government's dalliance with men and traditional leaders denied women access to land on the basis of culture and customary law, whilst using colonial racial policies to deny women access to land as black people. Post-independence policies, whilst attempting to address the racial imbalances, have largely failed to address the gender divide in access to land. As the land question continues to hog the limelight, the country must embrace human rights and constitutionalism and create laws, policies and practices that give women power to positively contribute towards the development of their country. That power should be economic, through access to land and other resources, political through participation in the governance of their country, and social through accepting the role of women as leaders and rightful land owners in families, communities and the country as a whole.

7.2 International Human Rights Frameworks and Women's Land Rights

International law is critical in articulating human rights and ensuring the monitoring and enforcement of women's rights. Article 1 of the Universal Declaration of Human Rights (UDHR) states that 'all human beings are born free and equal in dignity and rights'. In line with this realisation, subsequent human rights instruments developed both at the international, the African continental and SADC regional level have addressed the rights of women specifically, and in particular their right to be treated on the basis of equality with men. Following the development of instruments such as the United Nations Covenant on Economic, Social and Cultural Rights and the United Nations Covenant on Civil and Political Rights, specific instruments were developed to address the rights of women at the global and regional levels. These instruments include the Convention on the Elimination of all forms of Discrimination Against Women (CEDAW), the Protocol to the African Charter on the Rights of Women in Africa (the Maputo Protocol) and the Southern African Development Community (SADC) Protocol on Gender and Development. These instruments address a variety of issues that were covered by this research including equality in marriage and family life, women's land rights and the right to equality and non-discrimination.

CEDAW in Article 14 and with specific reference to rural women and land emphasises the rights of these women to 'equal treatment in land and agrarian reform as well as in land resettlement schemes'. Rural landlessness is one of the major indicators or predictors of poverty. This is in line with the observations by FAO which has recognised the link between landlessness and poverty and hunger, especially in rural communities (FAO, 2019:19), hence the need to pay special attention to the land rights of rural women.

Article 19 of the Protocol to the African Charter on the Rights of Women in Africa speaks of the promotion of women's land rights by stating that State Parties must 'promote women's access to and control over productive resources such as land' whilst Article 18 (a) of the SADC Protocol on Gender and Development urges State Parties to 'end all discrimination against women and girls with regards to… property such as land and tenure thereof'. CEDAW also provides for the need to ensure that spouses in a marriage relationship have the same rights in respect of the ownership, management, acquisition, administration, enjoyment and disposition of property (CEDAW, Article 16 (h)). The rights of women to be treated equally with regards to access to, ownership of and control over land and other productive resources is therefore well enunciated in international law. In all land reform programmes, the government must therefore ensure women's equality in relation to access, control and ownership of the available land. In doing so, it must be borne in mind that women have been marginalised in land reorganisation initiatives in the country from the colonial to the post-independence period and therefore special measures specifically targeting women in the process must be employed. Rhetoric about women's rights to land is not enough, efforts must be seen on the ground that reflect the political will to ensure that women enjoy those rights. Such efforts must invariably include implementation of the legal provisions that guarantee women's land rights and the development of programmes that target women as land beneficiaries.

The international human rights and treaty monitoring bodies such as the Universal Periodic Review (UPR) and the CEDAW Committee help to ensure that Zimbabwe as a signatory to the human rights instruments abides by its treaty obligations and implements constitutional provisions protecting women's rights. This has included assessing Zimbabwe's commitments in relation to women's land rights. The 2016 UPR of Zimbabwe urged the country to fully domesticate all provisions of CEDAW,[1] and to continue with implementation of policies that include measures for equal opportunities for women's participation in the country's economic development.[2] These were amongst the 260 recommendations that were made to Zimbabwe under the 2016 cycle of the UPR, many of which addressed the issue of women's rights generally and women's rights in relation to land specifically. In relation to land, the government of Zimbabwe was commended during the UPR for having laws that allow women and girls to acquire and inherit land and other property.[3]

The work of the UPR was complimented by the 2020 CEDAW report on Zimbabwe, with its specific focus on women's rights and gender equality. The Committee welcomed Zimbabwe's efforts in promoting access to land by women through S.I 53/2014, in particular the provisions of the instrument addressing spousal land registration and the establishment of the Zimbabwe Land Commission.[4] It however raised concerns regarding

---

1 Report of the Working Group on the Universal Periodic Review 2016, Zimbabwe, Para 131.21.
2 Report of the Working Group on the Universal Periodic Review 2016, Zimbabwe, Para 131.38.
3 Report of the Working Group on the Universal Periodic Review 2016, Zimbabwe Para 26.
4 CEDAW Committee: Concluding observations on the sixth periodic report of Zimbabwe, 2020, Para 43.

harmful practices that impede women's rights to inherit land despite legal and constitutional provisions supporting inheritance by women and girls.[5] The Committee also called on Zimbabwe to:

> Expeditiously complete a comprehensive and independent land audit to ascertain land ownership patterns, expose inequalities in land redistribution and release land for redistribution to women, as well as improve the allocation of resources to the Land Commission to enable it to implement its mandate fully and expeditiously.[6]

This was a noteworthy observation. As I have shown in this book, the land audit plays an important role in ensuring access to land by women under the country's land reform programme. The government of Zimbabwe as I have pointed out, has through the ZLC begun to implement the land audit,[7] and the expectation is that the process will be comprehensive, will be independent and transparent and in the process assist access to land by women. The focus must be on ensuring that the bulk of the land to be made available through the land audit is redistributed to women, in order to address the current inequalities.

The Committee also called on the country to 'facilitate access by women to their inherited land and penalize any action impeding or preventing them from enjoying their right to land'.[8] This was another important recommendation in relation to women's land rights given my findings that despite laws that allow women and girls to inherit land, there still remain pockets of resistance, informed mainly by harmful practices and invisible power that fails to recognise women's equal rights to inherit, own and control land.

The government should therefore pay attention to these conclusions, observations and recommendations from international treaty and charter bodies to ensure the protection of women's land rights in the country.

---

5 CEDAW Committee: Concluding observations on the sixth periodic report of Zimbabwe, 2020, Para 43.
6 CEDAW Committee: Concluding observations on the sixth periodic report of Zimbabwe, 2020, Para 44 (a).
7 'Land Audit gets underway', *The Herald*, 22 October 2018
8 CEDAW Committee: Concluding observations on the sixth periodic report of Zimbabwe, 2020, Para 44 (b)

7.3 The 2013 Constitution – Assessing the Potential

Tied to the international human rights framework is the country's 2013 Constitution and its progressive provisions on protecting women's rights generally and women's land rights specifically. It is therefore a good starting point with which to address the human rights challenges faced by women in relation to access to land. Fundamentally, in terms of the Constitution every person has the right not to be treated in an unfairly discriminatory manner on various grounds, including those of custom, culture, sex, gender, marriage or marital status; grounds that are often used to discriminate against women. Implementing the constitutional framework fully and unequivocally will therefore guarantee that:

i. All discrimination against women with regards to access to land is eliminated;
ii. Women are treated on the basis of equality with men; and that
iii. Women's prospects of accessing land are promoted.

There is in this regard an immediate obligation on the part of the state to embrace these principles and guidelines and ensure their implementation in order to ensure both immediate and progressive realisation of women's land rights in the country. Any further delays in addressing these challenges will result in the entrenchment of existing inequalities and this will only make it increasingly difficult to disentangle without serious contestations, for as each year passes, the current land occupiers further establish their positions.

The marginalisation of women in land reform has been a recurring problem in the history of Zimbabwe. It is therefore imperative for government to start showing commitment to addressing this anomaly, using its commitment to constitutionalism as a basis for action. Researchers have concluded that often gender concerns are incidental in the thinking of the Government of Zimbabwe (Essof, 2012:43). In the case of the FTLRP, the fact that as the country embarked on a new phase of land reform at the dawn of the new millennium in 2000, there was little to show that its attitude in relation to access to land by women differed from its immediate post-independence attitude. To address this challenge, government must therefore unequivocally show its willingness to embrace women in its land reform agendas. The 2013 Constitution provides a strong basis for this approach. It must be used as a framework for revisiting the FTLRP and assessing the challenges that women have faced with a view to addressing those challenges from a constitutional and human rights perspective. The creation and strengthening of laws, regulations, policies and institutions to operationalise the progressive constitutional provisions on women's land rights will be a useful and necessary approach to provide guidance to government officials and other actors in their implementation of land reform, resettlement and related programmes.

7.4 Power and Decision-Making

Power and decision-making are some of the critical determinants in relations between men and women. Under the FTLRP, these were manifested at different levels of the social, political and economic strata from the family to national level and institutions in between. The influence that the various actors had, and their ability to influence the actions and decisions of others, and even sometimes their failure to make decisions or take actions was of particular disadvantage to women. Their generally subordinate position meant that by and large, they could not effectively participate in the FTLRP and they were not fully involved in decision-making at the family, local community, provincial or national level in policy making and implementation. The result was a programme that marginalised women due to their lack of input on the preferred models and modes of the FTLRP. Negative power and its coercive and restraining nature was prevalent throughout in that those who wielded power used it to maintain their control over the marginalised by directing them on what to and what not to do whilst ensuring that there was no visible antagonism, opposition or threat to their power.

The seriously polarised, violent, and incongruous manner in which the programme was implemented meant that power was used as a tool of coercion and alignment. Negative power was used to command compliance and suppress independent decision-making especially against women who lacked power at the family, local and national levels. The absence of positive power and the inability of the majority of women to demand an inclusive programme also impacted negatively on levels of access to land by women.

How then can power and decision-making be used positively in land reform, access to land and access to resources programmes to ensure equal access to land by women? One way is to ensure that the state and its institutions guarantee the inclusion of women in positions of power and their participation in decision-making in public bodies. This is important because these institutions are responsible for policy formulation and implementation. Women's participation in these institutions ensures greater probability of specific issues that affect women being taken up in the public domain as matters for legal and policy formulation and implementation.

Article 7 of CEDAW enjoins State Parties 'to take all appropriate measures to eliminate discrimination against women in the political and public life of their country' and, particularly to ensure that women are able 'to participate in the formulation of government policy and the implementation thereof'. In the same vein women must be able to hold public office and execute all public duties at all levels of government. Similar provisions are contained in the Maputo Protocol[9] and the SADC Protocol on Gender and Development.[10] Section 17[11] and 80[12] of the 2013 Constitution supports this position, giving government a strong framework for taking a course for women's inclusion in decision-making.

In relation to women's power and decision-making at the family level, the international and national legal and human rights frameworks recognise the need for equality in marriage and family life. The family is viewed in international law as a fundamental building block or unit and an institution for the development of society, hence its recognition in founding human rights instruments such as the Universal Declaration of Human Rights (UDHR). The Declaration states in part that:

> Men and women of full age, without any limitation due to race, nationality or religion, have the right to marry and to found a family. They are entitled to equal rights as to marriage, during marriage and at its dissolution.[13]

---

9   Article 9.
10 Article 12.
11 Section 17 (b) (i) provides that the State must ensure that 'both genders are equally represented in all institutions and agencies of government at every level'.
12 Section 80 (1) enjoins the State to recognise that 'Every woman has full and equal dignity of the person with men and this includes equal opportunities in political, economic and social activities'.
13 Article 16 (1).

The recognition of the family as a paramount institution must go hand in hand with the rights that accrue to the parties to a marriage during the subsistence of the marriage and at its dissolution. State Parties and society at large are urged by the UDHR to protect the family. This is necessary to ensure that the family unit thrives and that its success helps in building cohesion in society and the nation at large. In line with this understanding, the Constitution of Zimbabwe requires the state to ensure protection of the family, including equality of rights and obligations of spouses during the subsistence of a marriage as well as at its dissolution.[14] Reality, however, shows that the responsibilities and obligations to protect the family unit have been unduly placed on women as opposed to the state, men and society, with the result that women are forced to endure violence, unfair treatment and discrimination within the family unit with the sole goal of protecting the integrity of the family unit.[15] This has negative implications on the women's well-being, mental and physical health and even impacts their ability to develop socially and economically. This in turn entrenches their dependence on the abusive men for their economic and social needs.

I have shown in this book that other aspects including lack of resources and traditional and cultural practices, forced women to accept a subordinate role in decision-making and access to land in marriage relationships. At face value, women appeared contented with mere access to land and being able to grow crops and feed their families. In reality however, women also wanted land that they could control and make decisions about in relation to use of both the land and the agricultural produce. However, because of the powerful positions of men as the economic providers and the customary imperatives that elevated men as the leaders of the family, women could not contest decisions such as registration of the offer letters, leases and certificates of occupation in the names of their husbands. To address this, government must double up on its efforts to compel joint registration of offer letters, leases, permits and certificates of occupation, including in retrospect, under the FTLRP as a way of empowering women in marriages and securing their access and

---

14 Section 26 (c).
15 Statements such as '*ndogarira vana vangu*' (I will stay for the sake of my children) are often used by women in abusive relationships in Zimbabwe to explain why they do not leave.

control over fast track land. Such joint registration must give equal rights and obligations between the spouses in relation to the land, instead of giving careful consideration to the rights of one of the spouses, especially at divorce as S.I 53/2014 provided. Instead fairness and equity must be the guiding principles in dealing with the land rights of spouses during the subsistence of a marriage and at its dissolution. Sec 7 (4) of the Matrimonial Causes Act is a notable starting point, with amendments to ensure that it applies to all types of marriages in the country, including unregistered customary law marriages.

7.5 Towards an Inclusive Access to Land Approach

Access to fast track land under the FTLRP was premised on criteria and practices that excluded certain segments of the citizenry. Access was determined by sex, gender and cultural biases amongst other considerations resulting in many women being elbowed out on the basis of their sex and/or gender and the attendant customary norms. In addition, access was also determined by one's political affiliation and position in relation to such hierarchies as well as social, economic and familial ties with influential individuals in the land reform process. Such considerations had the effect of disadvantaging women as they were not found in big numbers in any of these segments. Despite the political pronouncements by government and other leaders, which suggested that all people were free to access land, the reality showed that many women were left out because of the above considerations.

Women in the Chivi communal lands, one of the main catchment areas for the farms in Masimbiti in Mwenezi and the sugar-cane fields of Chiredzi District told me during fieldwork that they were still keen on accessing land, many years after the programme was initiated. This was because the initial programme had excluded them due to lack of resources, knowledge and know-how, plus the belief that they could not get the land unless they knew someone senior in party or government circles amongst other challenges. For the women who acquired land in the low value A1 allocations, many of them also wanted to get land in the lucrative sugar-cane plots in Hippo Valley and Triangle Estates in Chiredzi District but failed to do so because of the more stringent requirements for such allocations which had the effect of excluding them. Lack of access to information, lack of resources, limited levels of education and lack of understanding on how to complete the application forms for A2 allocations all had the effect of excluding women. The unclear and unsupportive legal and policy framework, violent nature of the FTLRP and power structures that did not work in favour of women, all worked to disadvantage women under the programme.

To address these challenges, government needs to develop laws, policies and practices that identify causes of exclusion for women in access to land and provide solutions for removing such exclusion. In addition to the recommendations given in the above sections, such policies, laws and practice guidelines for implementation must include the following:

i. Active identification of deserving but previously excluded beneficiaries, including women, the landless, communal area inhabitants and the provision of clear criteria for access;

ii. Provision of resources for resettlement such as schools, hospitals, water and sanitation as well as finances for agricultural production and criteria for accessing such resources as a prerequisite for resettling people;

iii. A clear outline of application procedures and how government can provide assistance in the application process for citizens in need of such help in an easy to understand format; and

iv. A transparent selection process that focuses on set criteria with limited discretion being given to those with the responsibility for selection of beneficiaries and allocation of land, in order to stamp out corruption, favouritism, nepotism and cronyism amongst other vices.

Whilst putting in place criteria for identifying beneficiaries and allocating benefits including land, farming inputs and finances may be considered as a perpetuation of the exclusionary practices, this is necessary in the context of identifying the normally marginalised members of society. In a free-for-all environment, these people are likely to be elbowed out of resource allocation and access processes. Without adequate protection and consideration from the state, women were left out of the FTLRP, and leaving them to fight for land in a murky and convoluted system will not address women's land rights. Certainty and giving specific attention to women's land rights and needs will guard against available land and other resources being snapped up by the privileged and those with the requisite social, financial and political capital. This approach is also necessitated by the realisation that without pro-poor and pro-women interventions, these social groups are unable to influence social policy and resource allocations due to their general marginalisation.

7.6 Conclusion

Perhaps one of the key lessons for policy makers emanating from Zimbabwe's FTLRP is that there is no substitute for planning, and a government that is in control particularly when implementing programmes of the magnitude of the FTLRP. There were arguments that the way in which the programme was implemented was the only possible way given the resistance by the white commercial farmers to provide suitable land or to provide any land at all for resettlement during the first two decades after independence. Some commentators have argued that Zimbabwean women were better off identifying with Zimbabwean men as blacks in taking land from the former white farmers than to concentrate on their needs as women during the FTLRP.[16] The commentator believed that it was going to be easier for women to get the land from black men once that land was in their hands as black people. The common 'enemy' then was the white commercial farmer and the primary battle was to take the land from the white farmer, after which a secondary battle by women to take land from men would ensue.

Twenty years after the commencement of the FTLRP, the question remains whether the secondary battle by black women to take over land from black men has started and whether there are any chances that such a battle will ever be fought and won? At what level has that battle been fought or will be fought? Will it be between the women of Zimbabwe and the State, the women of Zimbabwe against men generally or the women of Zimbabwe against the men in their families? This still remains to be seen.

On a different level, the ongoing land audit could provide an opportunity for women to access land. The sad part is that to date, government has not stated as a matter of law or policy that women will be prioritised in the allocation of land identified for resettlement through

---

16 View expressed by one of the lecturers during a PhD seminar at SEARCWL on 22 October 2010

the land audit, despite recommendations from key institutions such as the CEDAW Committee. The Supreme Court decision in the case of *Chombo v Chombo* also provides a positive direction with regards to women's access to land held by their spouses during marriage and at its dissolution. However, government must, in addition put in place mechanisms for women to access land in their individual capacities and not on the basis of their marriage relationships. This has become a significant point of consideration following the Supreme Court Judgment in *Chigwada v Chigwada*, where the court has emphasised the rights of spouses to will away their property to whomsoever they wish and exclude their spouses from inheritance in the process. The will making process can therefore be used to disinherit women of fast track land registered in their husband's name or where there is joint registration, of the half share that is held by the husband.

This I conclude, will be an indicator of government's indubitable commitment to women's rights and gender equality in accessing land as provided for in the country's Constitution. As things currently stand, the struggle for Zimbabwean women to be treated on the basis of equality with men in accessing land in the country continues. It is *aluta continua*.[17]

---

17 Portuguese for 'the struggle continues'. The phrase was used by the Mozambican liberation movement, FRELIMO during that country's war of independence. Zimbabwe's war of independence was largely waged from Mozambique (and Zambia) and therefore the freedom fighters of this war too adopted this phrase. I use it here to signify the continuing fight for land for Zimbabwean women, given the centrality of land in the country's war of liberation. Without the land, Zimbabwean women remain in bondage.

www.ingramcontent.com/pod-product-compliance
Lightning Source LLC
Chambersburg PA
CBHW051615230426
43668CB00013B/2111